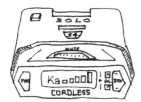

Portable Radar Detector $70 - $300 USD

Any car radar detector would be adequate. When ET is sending a transmission it makes a very different and distinct sound than if it's in regular operation while you are speeding down the highway. Set them to either highway (more sensitive) or city (less sensitive). If you have more than two, do some testing in advance to make sure they don't affect each other. In the field, don't aim their lenses toward each other as it may generate a false positive. Try the S4 unit: https://www.escortradar.com/solos4/. Or try http://www.radarsource.com.

Gamma Scout Geiger Counter $100 - 440 USD

Good for picking up radioactive radiation and may detect unseen extraterrestrial craft or traces of a landing. ET may also use it as a communication tool. It will chirp randomly while it's operating, but will double up to two chirps to say "Yes," or go silent if the answer is "No." The rechargeable version only needs charging once in three years. https://www.gammascout.com/collections/geiger-counters

Portable Lightning Detector: $26 - $499 USD

A storm tracker is normally used for detecting lightning strikes up to 50 miles away. If the device suddenly detects a lightning strike, it may actually mean that an ET craft has suddenly appeared by emitting a powerful electrical discharge. At an April 2012 training in Marcos Island Florida, Deb Warren had the experience of seeing soundless ball lightning a few miles away, with the storm tracker not going off at all. Then, the next night, there was a lightning storm that started 25 miles away, approaching them to within one mile, with the storm tracker beeping at every bolt of lightning. The ETs were interfering with something the first night, and for the sake of comparison allowed a real storm to pass the following night. To buy: https://www.ambientweather.com/sptb2iy.html

Digital Outdoor Thermometer: $12.99 USD and up

Monitors the air temperature and humidity level during fieldwork. If the air temperature suddenly spikes, it may indicate that an ET ship is hovering directly overhead; even cooler, the group may be *inside* a dematerialized craft. Available pretty much anywhere.

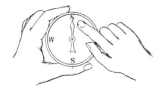

Compass ~$10 and up

A simple compass can be used. When affected, it will shift to point due south instead of north.

DEVICES TO RECORD SIGHTINGS

Do you know why most footage of UFOs is fuzzy, blurry, shaky, incomplete, etc.? Because it is so damn hard to get footage of a UFO, that's why. It's the middle of the night, you can't see anything, your gloves are on, you forgot which button does what, you can't even find the UFO in your viewfinder. When you do find it, you're not good at tracking it because you're so excited or because your camera is so zoomed in it's like looking through a microscope at lightning fast sky amoeba. As soon as the UFO goes out of frame (because you're shaking the camera, or getting lost trying to keep one real eye on it so you can participate in the sighting too), you have to find it again. I've personally given up on getting footage and trying to lead a group at the same time; it's too complicated. If you get as befuddled as me, delegate another person to it, or have a co-leader or group dynamic that allows you time to fiddle with equipment.

<u>Night Vision Video Camera</u>

Luna LN-DM50-HRSD ~$400 USD

- We have this one. It's handy to have the night vision and video recorder all in one device but it's very zoomed in so only a teensy fraction of the sky gets recorded. Using it is like shining a flashlight into one of your eyes, so adjusting back and forth between sky watch and documentation is somewhat challenging. http://www.lunaoptics.com/dm50hrsd.html

Bushnell Equinox Z ~$340 USD

- A night vision monocular with photo/video capabilities. It eats through batteries, but with an external battery like the Limefuel Blast L60X for $30, it lasts for hours and hours. http://www.bushnell.com/hunting/outdoor-technology/night-vision/6x-50mm-equinox-z

Digiforce X970 ~$760 USD

- This is the latest offering from the manufacturer Pulsar. Photo/video capabilities. It includes range-finding reticles. We don't know what that means, but it sounds good. http://pulsarnv.com/sku=PL78099

iGen 20/20 ~$399 USD

- You might consider this camera for a wider field of view. While lower in sensitivity than the X970 above, the iGen lens is threaded so that one can mount telephoto or wide-angle adapter lenses. http://www.nightowloptics.com/index.php (Click on "iGen" on the right)

Ranger RT ~ $900 USD
- We've heard some good reviews about the Yukon Ranger Pro, though it is discontinued. If you can't find one at the pawnshop, research the other night vision devices in the Ranger series sold by Yukon Optics. http://yukonopticsglobal.com/products/

<u>Infrared Camera $100 USD and up</u>

You can get a cheap Bell and Howell infrared camera from Amazon or eBay. Works well.
Search terms: "Bell Howell IR Night Vision Camera"

Traditional Camera

- You can use your regular camera to capture photos or video of UFOs. For best results use a camera with a high ISO.

- I once took several photos of the sky trying to figure out if one of the "stars" I was watching was moving in circles on me. I never figured out if I was imagining that or not, because after I got the photos downloaded to my computer I was much more interested in the bright red and white UFO that magically appeared in the frame. I was using my point and shoot, a SONY Rx 100 iii, Max ISO 128,000.

- Our CE-5 mentor Deb Warren has good results with her Canon D5 Mark 2 ISO 25,000. To see a sample of her photos, Google: "CSETI Joshua Tree jewel-like ET Craft."

- The famous Vero Beach Twin Ships video was shot with a Sony A7S. This line of cameras has remarkable low light capabilities, ISO 100,00 to 400,000.

Camera Specific to Capturing Orbs:

If taking pics of orb activity is your thing, older digital cameras that don't have 'hot mirror' technology (infrared filters) work best. Use a flash. In the book *The Orb Project*, the researchers used a Pentax Optio 330 and a Nikon Coopix 8800. Someone in our group uses the Canon PowerShot sd1100IS with good success. For tips on taking photos of orbs visit: https://orbwhisperer.com/orb-photography-tips.

Infrared Light $15 – 30 USD

A simple infrared light used at night helps you see orbs better when using your night vision goggles/camera or your regular camera or video recorder.

How to Capture Phenomena in Pictures

Some phenomena will appear in photos that you can't see when you are taking the photo. Any camera will do for this. Instructions:

- Make an intent to capture non-physical phenomenon and/or ET.

- Dusk is an especially good time to do this.

- Meditate, focus on communicating, feel the energy flowing.

- Then take random photos of area and sky.

- If indoors, try taking pictures of a dimly lit room with a flash. Aim for areas such as corners, as well as backgrounds that are not white as they will be easier to see when reviewing.

- Reputedly, a particular camera will get calibrated by your intent and will capture more phenomena the more you use it for this purpose.

PHOTOS

Here are some photos taken by people in our group and several contributors to this handbook:

Two anomalous grey shapes, Calgary Area, November 2016.

Anomalous energy unseen to the eye,
Lake Motosu, Japan, March 21, 2015.

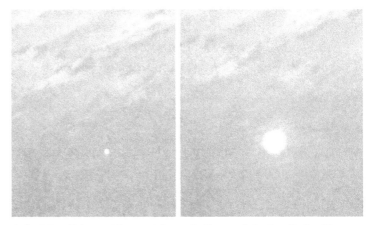

A flashing light on Mount Adams, before and during flash. There are no roads going up to this location. The magnitude of its brightness was also anomalous. ECETI, Washington State, May 2018. (Note: night-vision devices, such as the Luna Optics monocular used to gather this footage, records flashes and power-ups as brighter than they appear to the eye.)

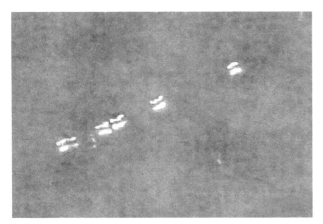

Five layered photos of a moving craft unseen to the eye,
Mt. Shasta, California, July 2016.

Multitude of orbs, ECETI, Washington State, May 2018.

Two UFOs travelling towards house, seen by multiple eyewitnesses. Volcano, California, November 2016.

Classic saucer-type UFO, Tokyo, Japan, November 2016.

Reputedly, UFOs sometimes hide as clouds. ECETI, Washington State, July 2017.

Horizon viewed *through* Keiko's head, ECETI, Washington State, May 2018.

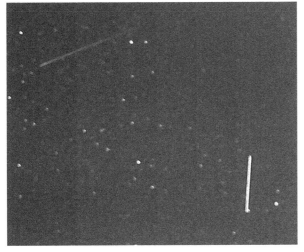

Streaker and a bright alleged satellite, Calgary Area, August 2017.

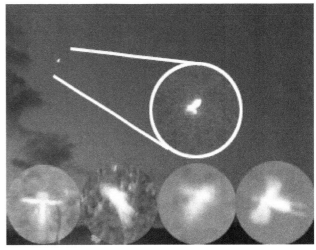

Anomalous lights, unseen to eye, ECETI, Washington State, May 2018, and Buffalo Lake, Alberta, July 2018.

INTERNAL COMMUNICATION

Because this experience is more about growth than about sightings, expect that you will have more internal experiences than external ones, especially in the beginning. This will be occurring not just during CE-5, but also during your dream state, meditation, and during your daily life. You'll know you're expanding when you feel better and better. The way you give and receive love will be unconditional, dependant only on your beliefs/state, and not on others/circumstances beyond your control. This section is notably shorter than the External Communications portion. Internal experiences are intimate, unique to each person, and usually impossible to fully convey. So here we keep it short and sweet and invite you to go within.

Very basically: Internal communication and interaction will come through your five senses. If you are new to your latent psychic ability then you will need some practice to start consciously being aware of these experiences:

- Clairvoyance: Seeing a vision, symbol, auras, energy, lights, etc. It may be in your mind's eye, or it may seem utterly real.
- Clairaudience: Hearing a voice, noise, sound, music etc. This may include ringing in the ears. It may be a word, a sentence or a downloaded package that you translate out. It may sound like your thoughts, "a voice in your head" or an out and out voice or sound.
- Clairsentience: Feeing something in/on/near the body—sensations, energy, touch, emotions, vibe, presence etc. Once again, may be subtle or concretely felt.
- Clairscent: Smelling something that others can't perceive.
- Clairgustance: Tasting something that others can't perceive.

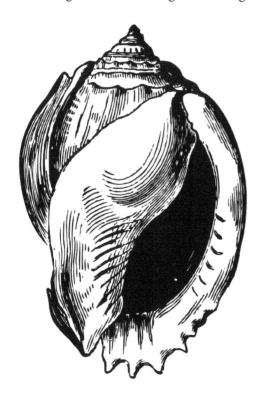

You may have several forms of psychic communication happen at the same time. You might have a full on interaction with a being. This might happen more easily in an alpha or theta brainwave state, in meditation, in your dreams, or in the state between sleeping and waking. You might have an experience that feels fully physical and real and then realize it's not when someone else cannot perceive it. Synchronicities may amp up. You may have body sensations indicative of energy downloads or upgrades or healings.

Practice your psychic abilities: when the phone rings, guess who it is. When you have a choice to make in your life, ask for guidance and go with your intuition. Get the ESP Trainer app. Learn more about lucid dreaming and invite an experience/ET to meet you there.

Specific Communications

Energy download:

> In the field, you may suddenly start to feel waves of
> energy flow up or down your body, which slowly intensify.
> Meanwhile, you may feel a tingling sensation in your
> fingertips and feet and/or muscle spasms in your torso. You
> may also feel slightly nauseous and have shortness of breath. All
> of these signs may indicate that you're experiencing some type of
> energetic download. If this happens, ground yourself. Give the
> energy a place to go. Plant your feet firmly on the ground, ideally
> with your shoes off. Or you can hold hands with other group
> members. Alternatively, you can hold onto a large crystal if you
> have one, or hug a big tree. Try to take deep breaths and stay
> calm and relaxed. It may feel unsettling and unpleasant but
> accept this energy as a special gift. It may mean you're
> receiving an energetic tune-up, a DNA upgrade, a chakra-
> clearing or a special healing. It might also mean your body
> is being used as a conduit to dispense high-dimensional
> healing energy into the earth. Whatever it is, you will enjoy
> a clear sense of energetic openness, awakening, and elation
> within a day or two. Some people have reported how this
> unique experience has permanently altered their life in a
> profound and positive way.

Merging:

> While in a relaxed, high-vibrational state, you may suddenly feel warm, fuzzy, tingling or
> blissful internal sensations slowly develop, move, and flow through your body. This may
> indicate that you're experiencing a merging; that is, a dematerialized being is interacting
> with your bio-electric field. It's a safe way for a being to confirm its presence to you on an
> energetic level. It's your decision though, by way of intention, to welcome and sustain
> this interaction or break it off. The choice is yours. The entity may also be expressing
> curiosity and choosing to explore, study, or connect with your physical and subtle energy
> bodies. There may also be a healing involved. For many, this connection is a unique gift.

"Is it my imagination or a real psychic experience?" The answer is not as important as what your
experience is; it holds personal meaning either way. However, as you get practiced you will get to
know the difference. When you become a really clear channel it will be obvious to you when
communication is inserted into your experience. If you are on a CE-5, don't be embarrassed, go ahead
and share your experience with the group whether you know the origin or not. In science you have to
be fearless. You can give them the caveat that you don't know. Your experience may be important to
someone in the group.

EXTERNAL COMMUNICATION

Alleged Satellites

All satellites are called "alleged" to indicate that we don't really know what it is unless proven. Satellites travel across the sky at a slow pace, and may sometimes flare as the sun reflects off equipment such as solar panels. NOSS, or NOSS-like satellites (Naval Ocean Surveillance System) satellites come in pairs or triplets. Discerning the veracity of satellites is a fun endeavour. Here are some points in the debate. Don't waste too much time on it or get too serious about it, since truly undeniable sightings are in your future.

- Satellites range in size from a cantaloupe to a large pickup truck, and orbit distance from earth ranges from 180 km to 35,000 km. What sizes of satellites can actually be seen with the naked eye?

- The International Space Station (ISS) is the size of a football field and only 400 km up. That is visible. (Not actually a satellite: it is a science lab with 3 to 10 astronauts residing inside it at any one time, cool huh?)

- An Iridium Satellite is the size of a truck, 780 km up, and is barely visible. (The first generation of these satellites used to produce a very visible flare. Sadly, the second generation, now fully deployed, are not expected to flare).

- Movement: Most satellites move in one direction: with the earth's rotation going west to east. Military ones move perpendicular to this: North to South (or South to North). There aren't many satellites that go east to west because it's more expensive to launch them in retrograde orbit.

- One way to find out for sure if a satellite is "alleged" or not is to ask it to power-up or change direction. Gather your minds and hearts and ask for it: groups have been answered!

- Some alleged satellites "wink" or "twinkle" brilliantly. It could be a satellite that is tumbling through space, reflecting the sun off of a shiny part. Or not.

- On some nights we see SO MANY alleged satellites; on some nights we see barely anything at all. We could try to dig into this more with a satellite app, but then again there's space junk. We gave up on this one and let the handle 'alleged satellite' speak for itself.

Alleged Meteors a.k.a. Streakers

- These are also called "alleged" because they can't be proven one way or the other. The most anomalous part about streakers is the high number of streakers that can occur on a CE-5 night. Ensure it's not a meteor shower night if you make this claim.

- There are so many variants of streakers: size, speed, color, distance travelled. On a retreat at Mt. Shasta we saw streakers that went across the whole breadth of the sky in a split second, large, thick, orange and green streakers, streakers that had a "wobble", and a streaker that was one shape that separated into two shapes at the front end.

- Streakers often appear at synchronous times, for example, when we're saying "Thank You" at closing, or when ET wants to highlight something someone says that they agree with.

Alleged Stars

"Alleged" stars will move in the opposite direction of all the rest of the stars. You will need a reference point like a tree to figure this out. They sometimes blink on and off, or twinkle different colours. Keep in mind that stars near the horizon do also twinkle due to refraction.

Flashbulbs

A 'flashbulb' is a quick flash of light that looks like someone up there took a photo of you with the camera flash on. It's quick! Whoever sees the first flash tells the group where the flash was and everybody focuses on that spot—very often there are more to come. Sometimes the flashbulbs stay in one place. Sometimes they move and keep moving, sometimes erratically, sometimes rhythmically, sometimes zigzagging, sometimes on course. We have twice seen a series of flashbulbs over 50 times, too many to accurately count. The first time, people actually got bored after counting more than 45 flashes and then went back to telling UFO stories while I was hollering "...48!... 49!...50!" I love my group.

Power-ups

A power-up starts out as an alleged satellite, low-flier, star or what looks like a plane. Then the light brightens, or a large bright orb flashes or "powers up" around it. A great example of a power-up is on Deb Warren's YouTube Channel: https://www.youtube.com/watch?v=OHC8X4j-i38. When watching footage, keep in mind that night-vision devices augment what little light is available, so the magnitude of a power-up is exaggerated compared to what we would see with the naked eye.

Low-flier

These are exciting sightings. MUCH brighter than anything else up there, these lights seem to be lower in the atmosphere. The ones we see travel across the whole sky, slowing to an almost stop at the edge.

Orbs

What are orbs? You have probably seen these spheres of light in photographs. The conventional explanation is that they are light refracting off of dust particles. However, it is odd that they can move against the wind, speed up, slow down, make turns, and seem to attend playfully to high-energy situations. They may be moving or stationary, and come in all colours and all sizes from teensy to gigantic. Some people can see them with the naked eye. Most people see them with night-vision goggles (ECETI is a great place to peek through multi-thousand dollar night vision goggles which James graciously passes around). Older digital cameras (without IR filters) can be used to capture orb phenomena either indoors or outdoors. Use a flash, but take care not to blind anyone in your group. (They won't be happy!) You can also use a simple infrared light to make it easier to see orbs either with goggles or when documenting digitally. Individually or a as group, you can also invite orbs for a picture—you may be surprised by how many show up for a photo op!

Probes

Little lights that come in close to the group. They may even show up inside the contact circle. They may also appear as small sparkling lights. They may be intelligent. They may be collecting information. They may just be saying "Hi."

Distorted Sky

A spot in the sky that looks like heat waves are moving through it, or a spot that is shimmering, that may have colours, or be darker.

Ruling out Human Machines

- Planes and helicopters have navigation and strobe lights, fly low, have limited speeds and manoeuvrability and make sound.
- Drones may or may not have a light, they emit a noise if you're close enough to hear it, have limited speeds and abilities, and are not allowed to fly very high. The last point may be irrelevant: people may fly them high regardless of laws.

The Real Deal: ET Ships or Military Space Craft (a.k.a. Alien Reproduction Vehicles, or ARVs)

The military is hiding their own spaceship fleet, reverse engineered from crashed UFOs. One of my friends married an above top-secret military specialist who saw one of these spacecraft at Area 51. (He recommends doing a Million Man March to the base to demand that we see what they are covering up, if anyone wants to organize that.) Can we tell the difference between an ARV and an ET ship in the skies? Probably not. We assume that the military isn't responding to our telepathic requests.

Both ARVs and ET Ships can:

- Can make a right angle turn, reverse, or stop and move again in ways that planes, drones and helicopters cannot.
- Make 'power-ups.'
- Don't have strobes.
- Have incredible speeds.

Our undeniable group sightings: At Mount Shasta at a retreat held by Kosta, a few of us saw about ten lights, in two perfect formations, tracking each other silently across the horizon. We've also seen a bright light move, stop, move, stop, and zip away. Another time we saw a light flying so low it illuminated a cloud. That was a low-flier, and we have seen three more: extremely bright lights that pass over us, and then slow to an almost stop at the horizon. We also consider flashbulbs to be confirmed sightings.

Let It Go

Don't get too caught up in figuring out if a UFO can be "debunked" or if it is of an unknown or interstellar origin – if the evidence is not that compelling, why argue about it? Accept that it might be a craft and save your energy for undeniable experiences. CE-5 Facebook groups always attract a few ugly trolls... If you are the type of person who is mean to others if their discernment is questionable, you won't get many sightings. That's because "mean-ness" is a low vibration, and if you have a low vibration, you won't be able to access sightings very easily. Please don't be a bully.

"Why are we just seeing lights and not cool physical craft like saucers and triangle craft?"

Sightings of up-close UFOs have declined in recent years. Ask people for their childhood or long ago UFO experiences and you will hear amazing stories such as the ones in our group: a dodecahedron craft with the top rotating counter to its base, vast black triangles covering huge portions of the sky, a metal ship in the fog almost close enough to touch... old UFO sightings were rad!

Why mostly distant lights now? It may be a safety issue. ET may not be able to get too close because air space (Especially North American airspace) is extremely tight. I guess the military will shoot them down if they see them. Nice. It is possible that, from a safety perspective, many of the ships interacting with our groups may not be piloted by organic beings from the far-flung corners of the galaxy but programmed or operated remotely using advanced AI technology.

Meeting a Being:

To date, we have not had any direct interaction with beings during a CE-5 event but one in our group has met face to face with a being in his home. I also have a friend in my neighbourhood who is a native shaman who has stood face to face with a being on one of her visits to a sacred site in the tropics, with several witnesses. When my friend saw the being, tears started streaming down her face… the being gently backed away, slipping back into the jungle. It would be an intense experience for many reasons, perhaps among them deep relief, overwhelming feelings of love and/or a yearning for reunification with galactic families that we have been estranged from for too long.

The majority of us are not nearly as ready as a shaman is to meet a being. We naturally fear the unknown or the different, and on top of that we have been programmed by the media to expect Extraterrestrials to be hostile or evil.

Preparing the group for face-to-face interactions is a good exercise to do. Get really relaxed and into a focused state, and walk everyone through a visualization where each person meets a being. (See the meditations section for an example.)

Another good exercise is to visualize running into an ET as you go about your daily life. Imagine an ET around every corner, up or down the stairs, at the coffee shop, stuck in a traffic jam in the car ahead of you, etc. You can even adorn the walls of your home with pictures of ETs. By doing this, you're basically

preparing your mind to mentally and emotionally accept, without fear or anxiety, a physical encounter with an ET being. Your belief system is also being re-programmed to recognize that these little meetings are actually natural, normal, and prosaic. This strategy will help to release those deep unconscious beliefs that meeting a real-life ET is impossible.

On a CE-5, or in your daily life, you may notice some phenomena gently leading you up to meeting a being: hearing shuffling feet, feeling a gentle touch on your third eye or somewhere on your body, or hearing breathing. Beings may appear in non-physical, inter-dimensional form such as sparkly lights, orbs, energy shapes, dark or fuzzy shapes or they can be fully physical in nature. It is reported that a sense of deep love is usually present during these interactions, whether telepathic communication is present or not.

Other Phenomena Other Than Sightings:

- Temperature changes - your body or the environment may warm or cool many degrees.

- Pressure changes - most often felt in the ears. This may indicate an ET ship overhead.

- Weather changes - such as a decrease or increase in wind.

- Body shaking or vibrations, body aches or uncontrollable restless agitation.

- Hair on body standing up.

- Sounds - buzzing, clicking, humming, animals responding to presence of humans and ET.

- Feelings of love so strong people are moved to tears.

- Electronics/Lights spontaneously turning on or off, songs playing on devices by themselves.

- Clouds - shapes, colours, anomalous moving/coloured clouds.

Tips

- Encourage people to share sightings and phenomena when they happen. People are often shy and don't want to disturb the group. Reassure people it's beneficial to the whole group if they share, but if you feel like someone is too nervous, give the option to not share. It's not an obligation.

- Often people won't believe their own eyes—continually ask people if they've seen something that they aren't sure is real or not.

- Let people share even during meditation—you'll get the feel for when you say, "cool" and keep going with the meditation or if you stop the meditation to watch for more developments.

Don't Miss: Conventional Night Sky Phenomenon

- Constellations, stars, planets, International Space Station, Hubble Telescope, Northern Lights.

- Milky Way: go deep into the wild and see the gorgeous Milky Way.

- Atmospheric refraction: Stars on the edge of the horizon seen through layers of earth's turbulent air seem to "twinkle." Watch this video to see the interesting effects of refraction on the sun and stars. https://vimeo.com/188149183

Vikings Sailing Under the Northern Lights,
Gerhard Munthe, 1899

"Why are some UFO sightings so questionable? Why would they not be super obvious? What's with this 'alleged' B.S.?"
We believe that entry-level sightings are meant to be hard to discern. It's very accessible to us. Most of us have an ingrained fear of "Aliens." Seeing something and wondering if it's possibly human made, possibly natural phenomena, or possibly UFO is not so scary. Entry-level sightings also serve another purpose too: It is a bridge for belief. Was that possibly what I thought it was? Could I believe that it could be a UFO? It helps you go out on a limb and gently opens you up to this whole thing. It also weeds out the people who aren't ready—they easily dismiss it and never give it a second thought. So a large group of diverse people can all see the same thing and have very different interpretations. Life is all about having different experiences and creating the reality we choose to create. Entry-level sightings allow each to their own.

"Why do some people get to see something and I don't?"
It is often that people will be looking at the exact same spot in the sky and one person will see a very bright flashbulb repeatedly going off, and the person next to them can't see a damn thing. Or, you decide to leave the CE-5 and a few people who decide to hang back see something right after you leave. Super annoying. That's just the way it is. Maybe you're not ready, maybe it's just not the right time for you, or maybe you blinked.

Think about how a dog can hear things that we cannot. It's the same with sight: our physical eyes can only see a very teensy range (est. 0.0035%) of what exists in the electromagnetic spectrum. In the context of UFOs, the reality ETs originate from and normally exist in is different than ours and most of us can't see that high up on the vibrational scale. So they have to adjust down or we have to rise up. You can widen your range, as many have. With intention and growth, you will see things that previously you couldn't see. I used to be jealous of someone in our group who regularly saw lights and orbs around him. Now I see sparkles and little 'flashbulbs' around me regularly. In time, you'll get there too. Try to be excited for those who you're envious of when they see something that you wanted to see too.

"Did I just imagine that?" Maybe, maybe not. Worth it to report to the group.

"But maybe it was a trick of the eye?" Maybe, maybe not. Still worth it to report to the group.

> Note to the leader: you really need to get your directional voice practiced. I have seen things and been talking out loud to myself thinking we were all having a group experience and later found out that no one was listening to me and therefore most people in the group missed the sighting of the night! Be commanding: ask direct questions and get answers: "Look right there!" "Who saw that?" "Keep your eyes on this light - there is something different about it." As you get practised, you will have a sense for what's worth having more attention called to it.

MEDITATIONS

Meditating has many scientifically validated benefits:
- Relaxing and calming
- Decreases, stress, anxiety, depression, pain, insomnia
- Increases ability to think more clearly and quickly
- Thickens the cerebral cortex of the brain, improving memory and concentration
- Increases ability to sense
- Strengthens telomeres in DNA responsible for longevity
- Creates new neurons (up to 30,000 per month, an enormous amount of brain power)
- Increases brain volume (brains normally shrink with age)
- Shrinks the amygdala, the fight or flight part of the brain (wow!)

Meditating and CE-5
Meditating helps you connect to one mind consciousness. When you become empty (Or connect to everything—whichever way you want to think about it), you are in a pure state of consciousness that is unbounded by time or space. As such, communication to anyone, at any time and space is possible. Moreover, meditation serves as a tool to clear the channel and tame the monkey mind so that random thoughts don't interfere with or distort outbound or inbound messages. So, the more you meditate, the better you can telepathically communicate with our star friends. During a CE-5, we recommend doing at least one-eyes closed meditation to really focus internally and get into one mind consciousness.

Reading from This Chapter
This chapter has several examples of meditations/group exercises from contributors all over the world. You can take this handbook into the field and read aloud to your group.

Playing Recorded Meditations
You can play meditations for everyone on a device. (This way you can join in too.) There are meditations on the ET Contact Tool app, and you can convert any YouTube video online into an mp3 by searching for a converter in Google (like https://ytmp3.com/).

Channelling as a Group:
One member of our group was lucky enough to go on an energy activation trip to Egypt with Sixto Paz Wells. He asked Sixto for CE-5 advice. Sixto said that it's imperative to learn to channel ET communication as a group. To do this, he suggested meditating together with the intention of receiving messages. Then, after the meditation, share your experiences with each other. If someone gets a message that is clear and direct, that could be communication. When several people receive the same information, you will know that you have a corroborated message. The messages are always positive, and never a warning or about a catastrophe.

Your Meditations
Before looking at the sample meditations in this section, consider that the best meditation is one from your own heart. Making up your own meditation is easy. You can write it down ahead of time, or make it up on the fly with the group. Because there are lots of pauses during meditation for breathing and cultivating a nice chilled out vibe, there's lots of time to think about what to say next. If it's not so smooth or you mess up, you can all laugh, which also helps create the right atmosphere.

<u>How to Meditate</u>

Meditation is simple. It is FOCUS. You can focus on:
- Music
- Sound
- Intention
- Emptiness
- Connection to All
- Mantras
- Breathing
- A feeling, like appreciation
- A part of the body, like your heart centre
- The blue light essence of yourself in front of your third eye
- Inhaling pranic energy and exhaling it to your body

Start with 5 minutes every day, once a day for a month, and then move up to 5 minutes twice a day. Increase to about 15 minutes twice a day. On busy days, try to stick to the habit: sit down even if just for 5 minutes. 5 minutes a day is better than 20 minutes once a week. Don't be discouraged if you don't feel a change or effect right away. It takes time to get used to. Try binaural beats in the Theta range to help your brain relax into deep meditation. You might try something similar to meditation, like coloring, walking, playing music, or going for a drive. If meditation just isn't your thing, that's okay too. Although beneficial, it's not essential.

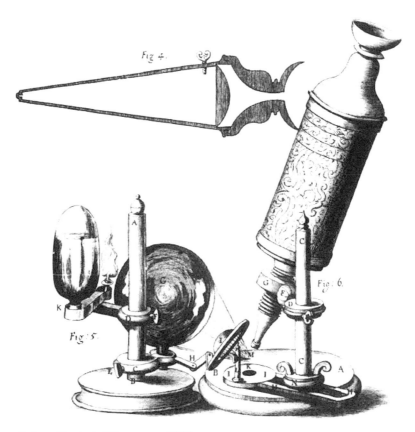

Robert Hooke's Microscope 1665

"There is far more evidence
that group meditation can
turn off war
like a light switch
than there is evidence
that aspirin reduces
headache pain."

—John Hagelin

The Group Advantage:

One of the reasons CE-5 works so well is because of the phenomenon of group meditation. There are several studies that show that when we meditate as a group, we are very powerful. Group meditation (a.k.a. the Maharishi Effect) has been shown to lower crime, suicides and deaths in surrounding areas between 13% to 82% (with an average of +70%) during the sessions.

Dr. John Hagelin is a quantum physicist and president of the Maharishi University of Management in Fairfield, Iowa. He says,

> "More than fifty demonstration projects and twenty-three studies published in leading peer-reviewed journals have shown that this new consciousness-based approach to world peace neutralizes the ethnic, political, and religious tensions in society that give rise to crime, violence, terrorism, and war. The approach has been tested on the local, state, national, and international levels, and it has worked every time, resulting in highly significant drops in negative social trends and improvements in positive trends. Large groups of peace-creating experts, practicing these technologies of consciousness together, dive deep within themselves to the most fundamental level of mind and matter, which physics calls the unified field. From that level of life they create a tidal wave of harmony and coherence that can permanently alter society for the better, as the research confirms. And this consciousness-based approach is holistic, easy to implement, non-invasive, and cost effective." (See http://www.permanentpeace.org for more information.)

Sunday Meditations

There are several groups around the world that meditate on Sundays visualizing peaceful change for the planet. To join one of these groups go to:

> http://www.globalunitymeditation.com/
> https://www.facebook.com/groups/128179887330632/ (We run this one!)
> http://2012portal.blogspot.com/2016/08/make-this-viral-weekly-ascension.html

Learn More:

> http://www.worldpeacegroup.org/washington_crime_study.html
>
> http://thespiritscience.net/2015/06/18/studies-show-group-meditation-lowers-crime-suicide-deaths-in-surrounding-areas/
>
> http://www.thewayofmeditation.com.au/blog/scientific-evidence-mass-meditation-can-reduce-war-and-terrorism/
>
> https://www.youtube.com/watch?time_continue=36&v=wJ0O1FTn9RQ

We want to mention as well that the numbers of groups holding meditation sessions around the world are growing. When minds and hearts collectively are focused on peace—on kindness to animals, international harmony, mutual respect, environmental preservation, prosperity for all, whatever you want for your world—the energy is exponentially magnified and brings closer each day the manifestation of those ideals. The value of prayer and active or remote participation in meditation groups cannot be overstated.

- Matthew's Messages, Feb 14th, 2018

Vision of a New World (Dr. Greer)

Hold one another's hands and see that there is a perfect circle of light formed. Feel the deep peace within us, and the stillness and quiet. In your inner sight, become aware that there is a trans-dimensional interstellar craft that is around us and that we are within it. There are extra terrestrial beings meditating with us, and we see this beautiful ring of light as we hold one another. Interspersed amongst us are ET life forms shifted beyond the crossing point of light and they are holding hands with us. As we go together into this pure state of silence, we see deep within each of us a fountain of pure light: consciousness made into light. It rises up through our chakras empowered by the light of the earth and the power of Gaia and it reaches our heart level and then it rises up to our crown chakra and it bursts forward upward to the space above us. It makes a perfect column of light. First, each of us individually project these columns, and then our columns blend into one and this light goes from left to right around the circle and becomes one massive beam of celestial light going upward into space piercing the stratosphere. This light spreads out, our light and the goodness within the earth and humanity and our full potential of enlightenment spreads from this place to every star and every galaxy and every intelligent life form in the cosmos. We ask the Great Spirit that is infinite and boundless to facilitate this beautiful light as a beam going upward, to be a guide for civilizations capable of interstellar travel to come to this place on earth. Ultimately we see this beam of light enter into a vast interstellar center. It is thousands of miles in diameter in deep space. This is where the ambassadors from other civilizations gathered for millions of years for time immemorial. We see that they behold us clearly even as in our own mind we see them. We ask them that they join us here and in their thought essence they do. We see that they are sending back through us a cosmic light coming from the zenith of the heavens into this beautiful circle of people and through us to the earth, and the earth rings like a bell. With the resonance of this cosmic light, it reaches every man, woman, and child on earth and they see a new vision of a new world manifesting from within us into the physical earth. We ask the Great Spirit then that for every man, woman, and child on earth, that their heart and mind and their essence and spirit be awakened to the simple truths that we are one people in the cosmos and it is time for us to enter universal civilization and endless peace. We see all the secrets that have been held from humanity unveiled. The wondrous technologies that could turn the earth into a rose garden of peace and abundance brought forward for the good of humanity. We see all those forces on earth that are retrograde or resisting this transformed by the beauty of this vision. Now we behold this light becoming stronger, and we see crystallized in our mind, and our vision, a new world. It will be an endless and unbroken time of peace for hundreds of thousands of years. While first it can be an external peace, the reality is that it will evolve into the age of enlightenment and in the passage of time, every child born on earth will be born in cosmic consciousness and hence evolve in God consciousness and universal unity consciousness. As humanity evolves in this fashion, we see that we become ambassadors to other planets, spreading enlightenment from earth even as enlightenment has been brought to earth by the ancient ones before us.

Our hearts are filled with joy at this vision and we ask that Great Spirit assist us in making it so and we invite these interstellar civilizations patiently awaiting our arrival to assist us as we vow to assist them. The children on earth will be the entry points for the channels, to which this knowledge and vision and reality manifests on earth. And so we ask the Great Spirit that this beautiful time, which we know in our hearts is the destiny of humanity, be bought forward. We dedicate ourselves with one another and with the earth, and with space, and with all these visitors, our brothers and sisters, of every star system, to create a new world, and we see that it is actually already born, within the realm of ideas, and it is ready to be made manifest, requiring our action. So with some effort on our part assisted by the Great Being and the unseen realms and the spirit world, and these interstellar civilizations, what seems impossible becomes inevitable. We will see it made manifest within our lifetime, and our hearts are filled with love and joy at the vision of a new world. Namaste.

Global CE-5 Initiative (Kosta)

1. Do this ET Contact any time, anywhere that is convenient, comfortable and safe for you.

2. Choose the place and the people you believe are compatible, respectful, and enthusiastic about this coordinated effort. As "vibrational beings", fear or other strong emotions can affect your results.* Bring your goodwill, love, joy and openness to the experience. The ETs will "pick up" on your noble positive vibrations. You can also do this alone.

3. Link heart-to-heart with members in your group. Circulate the love energy.

4. Imagine a sphere of love at the center of your circle with each of your hearts connected to it. Project this column of love energy high up into the sky as a brilliant vibrant beacon to our Star Friends.

5. When you go into meditation, in your imagination link up heart-to-heart with all of the other Global ET Contact groups who are joining in all over the planet. Then with love also include our Star Friends as you invite them and guide them to your location.

You can guide them to your location by projecting your consciousness out to them and visualizing how to travel from the location of our sun in our solar system to our Earth. As you approach it in your imagination, zoom in closer and closer to your specific location on the surface. Show them the images of where to find you!

6. Mentally and with your heart, ASK our ET friends what you and we can do in cooperation with them to bring about a healing for our planet Earth. Invite them to take more of a part in our Human affairs, recognizing that it is nonetheless Humanity's responsibility to solve its problems.

7. Remember that ET Contact can come in many forms. It may be a sighting of a Star Craft, a lucid dream, a telepathic message, a touch on the shoulder or knee, weird electrical phenomenon with communication devices or lights, and so much more.

8. Afterwards, please add your CE-5 Event Experience to the ET Let's Talk report archives!

*NOTE: How you approach your CE-5 Experience is CRITICAL. If you have an attitude of fear, deep skepticism, hostility, close-mindedness …
chances are good you will fail at making contact.

Universal One

Close your eyes and take three deep breaths, exhaling with a sigh each time.

Continue focusing on your breath: with each inhale, breathe in the light energy that surrounds you. With each exhale release all the worries of the day, the struggle of survival, all the stress and negativity... Nothing to do, nowhere to go, nobody to impress. Inhale peace, exhale release.

Listen for the wind in the trees (Or the drone of traffic, or the hum of electricity, depending on where you are). Expand your awareness outward to include your friends beside you, the trees and animals around you, the people in cars on the highway beyond, the busy cities and countries far away. You are every person and every thing, and you can feel what it is like to be driving down the highway, to be a child playing in the park, or to have your leaves rustle in your treetop.

Your awareness expands farther, including vast tracts of land and oceans, into space, embracing our solar system and infinity, where you can hear the deep hum of planets revolving around their suns, feel galaxies spinning, and see soft coloured nebula clouds. You are vast, deep space... you are the wonders of nature: planets, moons and stars, forests, waterfalls and tides, inhabitants of worlds. Hear both the wind in the trees nearby and the music of the universe. You are everything and everyone.

Collapse this awareness into the space directly before your third eye. Strip away your personality, your individuality, the distractions of your environment, your thoughts. You are in the void, floating in the dark. You are original awareness. You feel the peace of infinite love... you are ultimate reality, which is bliss.

Thoughts and images may come through, and you let them go and return to this single point of focus and awareness. You have become the single point of awareness that is the same awareness that is felt by every other person on earth, every other awake and conscious being. You relax into this quiet awareness as it equalizes you and connects you to universal one.

Every Moment is a Meditation (Matt Maribona)

Matt discovered how to make contact with ET by himself many years before finding the CE-5 community. His example shows us that each of us can find our own unique path to contact.

CE-5 is not just a term; it is a practice of love, togetherness and integrity. CE-5 is all about being the unique, loving and joyous YOU. CE-5 is just the beginning of an amazing journey that will help change the world as we know it. CE-5 meditation should have no beginning or end. CE-5 is simply about being. Out there in the universe are an infinite possibility of wonders. Within the galaxies and stars and planets are other unique, loving and joyous beings just like us, that are simply being. They are out there waiting for us to realize just how special our world and all life truly is. THEY come from across the vastness of possibilities to shine great light upon you. All we need to do is join together and shine that light upon our world and ourselves.

Each day as we wake up we should be manifesting good into each of our lives. Our thoughts are very powerful and can be used to create the very reality that we live in. Everything is consciousness. We are creating our very realities with these thoughts. We are essentially what we think. As a species collectively, we can create a world that honors love for all things. It starts with YOU.

Throughout the day and within ourselves we should be the change we wish to see in the world. We need to be kind to one another. We need to take care of our world and take responsibility for our actions. Smile more, lend a hand to a stranger, do good deeds, carry hope everywhere, show love to everything. This world is a paradise and everything is provided. Separation holds us back. Separation from ourselves, each other, the world and the universe. We are loved and all we need to do is just be. At the end of the day, when the stars come out to shine for you, all you have to do is just say, "Hello, I'm here because of love and hope." Your everyday life is the meditation. The heart that beats within you is all that matters. Once you find that heart center, all you need to do is just look up and say, "Here I am, would you like to join me?" That's it! When you make contact you will see that love is all that matters and everything that is done with love is done with the best of intent, an open mind and open heart. The more there are who are of the same frequency and vibration, the more profound the experiences will be. The more you shine your light, the more they will shine theirs back. They wait out there for us even now as you read this. You are loved. Show them some love in return. Do it together. Just be.

Golden Age

Take three deep breaths and release all the stress and struggle of your daily lives. Ground yourself to the earth and feel your connection to the diversity of Gaia, humanity, all beings in the universe and to Source. Take a few moments to center and settle into your true self. Breathe and deeply relax.

Now, join minds and hearts with all in the group. Envision the evolution and progression of humankind. Feel your awareness of the world as it is now, primed for the utopia to come. It is a gift and an honour to be in human form on this planet at this time. In your minds eye, see the smooth progress of the continuous dawn of the new era before us. See corrupt leaders and manipulators of the world peacefully stepping down, and being held accountable for their actions. See popular media released from the grip of control, releasing critical information to all. Witness the slow and steady disclosure of the presence of our star family. Cherish seeing hope and relief alighting on each person's face when they realize we are not alone. As the critical mass of people accept and embrace this new reality, see scientists working, unencumbered, implementing the technologies already gifted to us, distributing free energy to the world. See the world bathed in harmony and love. Delight in the abundance and peace that will be available for all.

Imagine what you will do in that new world. Envision war prisoners being released... slaves freed... sickness healed... the hungry fed... free energy for all... communication with beings from other worlds... what your home will look like... what your own personal spaceship will be like... vacations to the stars or all around the globe... what your day looks like... where you put your energies for work... and what you do for play... place your mind's focus on whatever sets your heart afire!

Open yourself to hear inspiration from your higher self about what action you can take to facilitate this change. Take a moment to listen for guidance on how you will most effectively participate in this joyful process.

Know that this beautiful vision of the future is coming; it's just a matter of when. Conjure feelings of appreciation and peace for this reality that already exists in timeless flow.

Meet a Being

Create an intention that your group will do a meditation where you meet a being in preparation for eventual face-to-face contact. Have the group think about what kind of being they would like to meet: Human like? Non-human like? Some to pick from: Pleiadians, Nordics, Apunians, Hathors, Lion Beings, Arcturians, Avian Beings, Benevolent Greys and Reptilians, etc.

Alternatively, they could meet members of the ET team assigned to your CE-5 group or their personal ET emissary.

(Fun fact: Paul Hellyer, one of Canada's past defense ministers, says that there are 82 alien species that are known to have visited the earth.)

Open the meditation with any kind of breathing or relaxing exercise. You can move through a muscle tensing and relaxing exercise, or you can use a visualization of getting on an elevator and counting down ten floors, getting more and more relaxed with each level passed. It's especially important to be as relaxed as possible while doing this meditation, so take your time on this part—make it about half of the whole meditation. The goal is to get as relaxed as the state we are all in just before we wake up: this is often the most relaxed moment in our day.

Once you have brought everyone into a deeply relaxed state, have each person create a safe place where they would like to meet an Extraterrestrial being. It could be a sacred place, a park, a meadow, the beach where Jodi Foster met her "dad" in the movie Contact, a Galactic Space Station, etc. If you use the elevator technique, have the doors open into this safe place. As each person enters into this space, have them flesh out the details: the sights, the sounds, the smells, the ground under their feet. Have them walk to the place where they will meet the being.

Have each person create their invitation however they wish: a telephone call, a telepathic call, a written invitation, an email, etc. Visualize the being receiving the message and starting on their way.

Now imagine the first level of contact. Is it viewing a spaceship far away? Seeing the being standing at the edge of the far end of the beach? Sit with that for a moment. Acclimatize to it and continue to breath and feel deeply relaxed.

Now tell the group to ask the being to come closer. Give the group about five minutes to connect with this being at the pace that is most comfortable to them. Remind them to keep cultivating their state of deep relaxation. Point out to your group that each is in control of this interaction, and that they can ask the being to approach or retreat at any time. Tell them that if things feel uncomfortable or fearful, to breathe into the feelings and allow those feelings to melt away, replacing them with trust, love and appreciation.

After the time has elapsed, instruct the group to wrap up their communication with the being.

Have them thank the being and listen for the being's response. As the being moves away, remind the group to continue with that feeling of relaxation. Ask them to take note of how they are feeling: are they impressed at their ability to manage their own emotions and allow this interaction to happen? Are they feeling appreciation for what they feel is a representation or real interaction of benevolence and love? Let them bask in the warmth of this interaction after being is gone.

Now, gently bring each person back to our shared reality. If you did an elevator ride, go back up the floors, feeling more awake as you pass each floor. Invite people to wiggle fingers and toes if they would like, and or to take a few deep breaths as they acclimatize back to your location.

The Hathors assisted the people of Ancient Egypt. This representation is from a musical instrument, 664 – 525 B.C.

Quick and Dirty CE-5 Meditation (Deb Warren)

This meditation can be found at: https://www.youtube.com/watch?v=spkk6TwWpzg&feature=youtu.be

1. See a large golden ball of energy forming at your heart chakra, getting bigger and brighter, then it moves from left to right around the circle, in a counter clockwise direction, going through the heart chakra of each person present. It spins faster forming a golden ring, and our group starts to feel more coherent, then it spins even faster flattening out to a golden disc, and we start to feel even more coherent– we are a group taking this journey together.

2. Now as a group we begin chanting the mantra: Im Na Ma. Im Na Ma, Im Na Ma, while forming the Merkabah tetrahedron in our mind. And the disc now pops out to a golden ET craft, which surrounds all of us. It begins to gently float up carrying our astral/light bodies, and comes to a stop just above us.

3. And now … we hyper-jump.

4. We are now in geo-stationary orbit high above our location on earth. We can still see the sun shining on the Pacific Ocean in the West. We can also see the earth turning into darkness in the East. A sliver of the moon may be visible [localize these instructions for your area]. Look for the planet Saturn, like a very bright star, it may be to the left [or right] of the sun, that is our destination.

5. And now… we hyper-jump.

6. We are now above the rings of Saturn, and we can see a large ET space station in orbit between the rings and the planet. The space station is 26 miles long and many stories high. Our ET craft is gently heading toward a very large hangar deck. There are many, many ET craft coming and going from the deck. We enter the hangar, and look for a place to land our golden ship. We land gently and the golden ship fades away.

7. This place is like Grand Central Station. It is chock-full of many, many beings, all coming and going. We are surrounded by throngs of beings. Many different species. No one seems to notice our arrival, and we don't know where to go next.

8. We convene as a group, standing silently. Sending this telepathic message: we are humans from earth and this is the first time we have come to this space station. We need help. Please send someone to guide us.

9. Almost immediately, we can spot a group of ETs, making their way through the crowd. Soon they are directly in front of us, beckoning with a finger, indicating that we should follow them. We do.

10. We are taken to a side room on the hangar deck, and a door swooshes closed, and suddenly the noise from outside is no longer and it is quiet. There is at least one ET here to interact with each of us, and there may be more than one for each of us. You can ask for a tour of this space

station, you can ask for explanations and display device will be produced to help you understand. You may be asked to go to a large meeting room and make a presentation. I will give you a few minutes now to have these experiences, and no matter how time-consuming your experience is, these few minutes will be all the time you need.

11. I will be silent now while you have your experience.

12. Note to Facilitator: wait a few minutes. You will sense when everyone has finished their experience, and then you will begin the return trip back to Earth. Make sure that you also have an experience on the ET Space Station.

13. Wherever you are or whatever you are doing make it your intent to return to the group who are waiting for you on the hanger deck. Say goodbye to the ETs, let them feel your gratitude, let them feel how delighted you are, let them know if you would be willing to return again.

14. We are standing in a circle, everyone has returned.

15. See a large golden ball of energy forming at your heart chakra, getting bigger and brighter, then it moves from left to right around the circle, in a counter clockwise direction, going through the heart chakra of each person present. It spins faster forming a golden ring, and our group starts to feel more coherent, then it spins even faster flattening out to a golden disc, and we start to feel even more coherent.

16. Now as a group we begin chanting the mantra: Im Na Ma. Im Na Ma. Im Na Ma. And the disc now pops out to a golden ET craft, which surrounds all of us. It begins to gently float up, carrying our astral/light bodies, and carries us out of the hangar deck, and comes to a stop above the rings of Saturn. We look for the pale blue dot that is Earth.

17. And now... we hyper jump.

18. We are now once again in geo-stationary orbit just above our location here on Earth, once again we see the sun shining on Earth, and now we consider the location directly below us.

19. And now... we hyper jump.

20. Our golden craft is just above our physical bodies and it is now floating down, returning our astral/light bodies to our physical bodies. And then the golden craft fades away.

21. When you are ready, take a deep breath, open your eyes and move your body to indicate that you have returned.

22. Everyone should be silent until all have returned.

23. When everyone has returned, invite people to comment on any experience they had during the meditation. No one is obligated to share. You may wish to ask if there was anyone in the group who did not have any experience at all. In the next event you will focus your attention on that person, ensuring that they are part of the group. You may ask others to focus on these non-experiencers as well.

Interplanetary Council

From the Book *Evolution Through Contact* by Don Daniels
To learn more about his book, as well as access other resources, go to Don's website at:
http://www.becomingacosmiccitizen.com/index.html

Sit comfortably in a firm or lightly padded relatively upright chair, with your feet separated and your hands in your lap, palms down. Take a series of at least seven slow, deep breaths, inhaling as slowly and deeply as possible, then pausing as long as you comfortably can, and then exhaling slowly and deeply, and again pause as long as comfortable.

Continue, focusing on your breathing, until you are in a deeply relaxed state. Now, visualize your breath coming in through the top of your head (like a Dolphin), flowing down through your entire body, and flowing out through the base of your spine and the soles of your feet when you exhale. Allow your breath to bring in pure love and compassion, and exhale any negative thoughts of emotions, in this way purifying yourself with each breath.

Now, start to focus on the pause between breaths, and you will notice that in the pause there is a moment of Deep, Profound Silence. Gently go into that silence, and allow it to expand longer and longer with each breath, until eventually the silence will fill the entire breath. Become aware of

awareness itself, not the stray sound that you may hear, but that by which you are able to hear that sound. In this way sounds will not be a distraction, but simply an acknowledgement of your connection to the fundamental awareness that infuses every conscious aware entity in the universe. Then let the sound go, and return to focusing on communing with the deep profound silence that starts between the breaths, for this is your connection with the Cosmic Consciousness, the collective consciousness of the Universe itself.

Now imagine yourself as a Dolphin at play in the ocean, leaping and spinning and diving, just for the pure joy of it. Revel in the joy of your perceptions and your freedom. Dive deeply into that sea of pure consciousness, and then swim upward as fast as you can, leap into the air, and just keep going, faster and faster up through the atmosphere, past the moon, past our planets and out of our solar system. See the stars passing faster and faster, until you are out in intergalactic space looking at all the beautiful galaxies around you. Commune with the deep silence, and contemplate what a beautiful universe Creator has wrought. Understand how we are all connected through that creation and through our connection with Cosmic Consciousness, and how we are all thus "One" with each other!

Now put out the intention that you wish to visit the Interplanetary Council, and allow your consciousness to take you in the proper direction. You can travel at the speed of consciousness, so you should arrive quite rapidly. As you approach, note your impressions of the craft or building. And now, ask permission to go inside. Most likely someone will guide you, or you may simply find yourself inside.

Greet any guides with respect and humility, explain that you are wishing to visit as a citizen representative of Earth, and ask if you may visit the council chambers. Enter with the same reverence as if you were attending a general assembly of the United Nations. You will most likely be ushered into the viewing gallery. From here, take in the look and feel of the chambers. How large is the room, what shape is it, how high is the ceiling, what are the walls like, and what materials does it appear to be made of? Is there a table or negotiation area, what does it look like? Are there any objects on the table or over it?

Now, pay particular attention to any of the diplomats that may be present.

What impressions do you get of them? Take note of their physical appearance, and also any emotional impressions or telepathic messages or impressions you might receive. You might find that you make a connection with one of the diplomats. Offer your willingness to help with the evolution of humanity to the point where we can become full galactic citizens. Now become perceptive of what impressions you get in return.

Now, give your thanks and gratitude for being allowed to visit, and prepare to take your leave. Allow your consciousness to move back outside, and rapidly fly back to our galaxy, to our sun, to our earth, and back to your body. Your consciousness knows the way and will not get lost. And now, slowly and gently begin to return to normal waking consciousness, becoming gradually more awake with each breath.

While everything is fresh in your mind, make notes of impressions, and put the notepad next to your bed. You will very likely find insights and inspirations flowing into your consciousness over the next several weeks, especially in the hypnogogic state when just falling asleep or waking up, so having the notepad handy will allow you to take notes as any impressions come flowing in.

Resonant Energy (CE-5 Aotearoa, New Zealand)

The basic intent of this meditation is to allow for greater exchange or download of subtle energies that often enter into the fieldwork of CE-5 teams.

Grounding is important and we recommend everyone have their feet on the ground during this process. Teams may also hold hands if they wish, or even stand close together in a circle for the guided portion.

Start with a general cool-down, ask the team to relax, take slow deep breaths, and centre themselves. Breathe in peace and calm, and allow any worries and concerns to flow out through your feet into the earth as you exhale. Ask Earth to take away and deal with any worries and concerns and help us to focus on our current intent. Breathe in through the nose and exhale through the mouth. Ask everyone to picture/imagine or simply "ALLOW", their energy-body/astral hands, to reach quickly down into the centre of the Earth, gather some of Earth's energy, and bring it up to the first Chakra. This can be as rapid as breathing out to send your request, and bring the energy up as you inhale. Usually, we do this THREE times for each Chakra before activating it, as this intensifies the feelings, however,

when people are very familiar with this it can be done once per Chakra. With the 3X method, for the first two HOLD or store the energy at the Chakra as you go back down for the next amount. On the 3rd pass, rapidly OPEN your first RED Chakra then relax as you observe it glowing, or spinning etc. Then continue to reach down as you exhale, gather more energy and bring it up next to the second Chakra, pulling the energy through the first as you do so [alignment]. Repeat this process until everyone has aligned and opened their Chakras RED-ORANGE-YELLOW-GREEN-BLUE-INDIGO-VIOLET.

Next, the RESONANCE of the group is matched by sharing these Chakra energies in sequence. Ask everyone present to pass the light of their 1st, Red chakra, to the person on their right, taking in from the left the equivalent energy from that person. Quickly repeat this, asking the team to speed up the procedure so that we form a counter-clockwise red ring of energy at that level. Move up to the second Orange Chakra and repeat this process. Continue until you reach the Crown Violet Chakra. Now the whole team has their energy centres resonating uniformly. This action should be extended to include OTHERS PRESENT [ET, Celestial, etc.] who are actively working with us. This means the resonance extends through BOTH teams. The Heart center is the major one but it's easy enough to talk the group through with this process added in before starting.

Once these chakra rings are established, the next steps are to establish a common single form through which energies may flow in BOTH directions.

Ask everyone to visualize the rings "collapsing down" so they all reside at the heart chakra level. From the crown down, and from the base upwards. This will form a toroid, allow it to blend and become a white ring of light, spinning counter-clockwise just as the initial rings were established.

Now send back down into the center of Earth, a CLOCKWISE spiral vortex from this toroid. This is a "guide" for what comes next. Ask Earth to send back to us a counter-clockwise flow of energy that twins with the vortex we just created; as it arrives see/imagine/allow it to start wrapping around the heart Toroid, following

around it tightly in the counter-clockwise direction like a coil. Now send upwards to whomever we are working with, a COUNTER-CLOCKWISE energy vortex also as a guide to be twinned. Ask them to reply by sending down a CLOCKWISE vortex matching the path of our guideline; as it arrives allow it to wrap around our toroid, running clockwise over and around. Allow it to "run" at whatever speed it needs in order to resonate.

This form is VERY POWERFUL and you may experience significant energy flows.

Ask the team to keep this "vision", this energy field, strongly within their thoughts as you move into the silent part of the meditation, in which you seek to fulfill the team's stated intent of CE-5 work. Allow the ET's/Celestial beings or whoever you seek to work with, to use this resonant field to interact with your team. Specifically invite relevant celestial/cosmic energy to be integrated/downloaded into the team through this process and resonant form, and ask all those who are willing, to absorb/merge with these energies, allowing them to be distributed in a useful way as a result.

MEDITATIONS: CLEARINGS

Energy clearing meditations help to raise your vibration and become more aware of ET communications of all kinds, internal and external. It can be as simple as blessing and thanking every cell of your body, or bathing yourself in the highest light. Smudging with sweetgrass or sage is very effective: it creates a dense, neutral charge, releasing negative energy as well as purifying yourself and clearing a sacred space. For a more comprehensive clearing, try any of these healings/clearings on the following pages.

Chakra Clearing

Instruction: Start with deep breaths. Get relaxed. Go through each chakra, one by one, following the list below. Start at the root chakra at the bottom and make your way up. For each chakra visualize it becoming brighter, lighter, more vivid. Breathe into each chakra and clear away any debris, tension, disharmony or immobility from each chakra. Read aloud the chakra's corresponding energy blocks and release the negative emotions and false beliefs associated with each. See in your mind's eye each chakra glowing powerfully and illuminating your body with its corresponding color. Feel the energy of the chakra freely flowing or spinning.

Root Chakra
Base of spine/pelvic floor/genitals - Red - Survival. Blocked by fear. Accept the feeling of fear and know ultimately fears are not real.

Sacral Chakra
Lower Abdomen/a few inches below naval - Orange - Pleasure. Blocked by guilt. Forgive yourself.

Solar Plexus Chakra
Upper Abdomen/above naval - Yellow - Willpower. Blocked by disappointments. Accept all learnings.

Heart Chakra
At your heart - Bright Emerald Green - Love - Blocked by grief. Accept and release loss and the life process. All things change and come and go, but love always stays and is an infinite energy.

Throat Chakra
Throat - Robin's Egg Blue - Truth - Blocked by the lies we tell ourselves. Face yourself and allow yourself to be perfectly imperfect, vulnerable, worthy.

Third Eye Chakra
The middle of your forehead, above your eyes - Indigo - Light - Blocked by illusion of separation. Allow insight and knowing that we are all one.

Crown Chakra
Top of your head - Violet - Pure cosmic energy - Blocked by earthly attachments. Let go of everything you have loved, knowing nothing ever truly disappears.

Healing Negative Influences/Clearing
(James Gilliland - ECETI)

Healing is a must for all those who desire to operate in other realms of consciousness. You must have self-authority and maintain control. If you are experiencing negative vibrations, they are either thought forms, limiting mental concepts, psychic bonds or discarnate entities (lost souls) in need of healing. They are bound to the earth vibration due to lower vibration attitudes and emotions. Some are coercive and desire to manipulate and control. Love heals. Casting out only sends them to another place, another person. In all healing, remember that God is love. It is the power of love that heals and lifts. We will give you the following steps to clear the energy.

1. Close your aura by visualizing a white or gold light around you.
2. Call upon your chosen cultural representative of God, be it Jesus, Buddha, Babaji, Mary, Mohammed, White Eagle or another one of the Beautiful Many Christed Ones.
3. Tell the entities they are healed and forgiven, lifted and enlightened.
4. Tell them they are healed and surrounded with the Christ light and the Christ love.
5. Ask your chosen representative to take them to their perfect place.
6. Ask that all negative thought forms and limiting mental concepts be dissolved and lifted in the light of truth.
7. Ask that all psychic bonds be severed, and close their auras to all but spirit of the highest vibration.

Repeat this process until you feel clear. There may be more than one healing to do. Remember your word is very powerful, and what is spoken on their level manifests instantly. Many enlightened ones use this process before opening. It creates a clear and safe environment, and it also lifts the one who is doing the healing. Intent is nine-tenths of the law. If you intend to serve and heal, you will draw to you entities of like mind. If you intend to coerce or manipulate, again you will draw entities of like mind. It is the law of attraction. At times, discarnate spirits will come to your light like a moth to a flame. Do not judge yourself, simply heal them. They are the ones in trouble, not you. They are seeking your help.

Short form of clearing prayer – after doing the above in the beginning. First call in your main teacher or guide and other divine beings Christed or above.

WE WELCOME ALL ENTITIES IN LOVE AND LIGHT

WE SPEAK TO YOU FROM THE LORD GOD OF OUR BEING

TELLING YOU ALL YOU ARE HEALED AND FORGIVEN

LIFTED AND ENLIGHTENED

HEALED AND FORGIVEN

LIFTED AND ENLIGHTENED

FILLED AND SURROUNDED BY THE CHRIST LIGHT AND THE CHRIST LOVE

AND WE ASK THE BEAUTIFUL MANY TO ESCORT YOU OFF TO YOUR PERFECT PLACE

GO IN PEACE

(See James' book *Reunion with Source* for Advanced Healing techniques)

Breathing In Earth Energy Cleansing
(Little Grandmother Kiesha)

Stand with your bare feet on the Earth. You can do this indoors as well, but take your shoes off. Start by breathing the color green, the color of Earth energy, up through the soles of your feet; feel this Earth energy filling your cells and nourishing every inch of you; with the first in-breath, bring it up as far as your knees, then exhale it down and out through the soles of your feet back into the Earth.

On the second in-breath, bring this green energy up to the base of your pelvis (first chakra), and exhale it back into the Earth, feeling it enshroud your thighs, your knees your ankles and back down through your feet. As you are doing this, if you have trouble connecting to any particular area of your body, and feeling the energy fill you, continue with the breaths up to that area until you feel ready to move on.

On the third in-breath, bring the energy up to your lower pelvis, just below the navel (second chakra), and release it back downward into the Earth. Be sure to focus on each particular part of your body as you descend the energy; do not just skim over but visualize and feel the energy travelling down and filling your limbs, your muscles, blood, bones, cells.

On the fourth in-breath, bring the energy up to your mid-belly (third chakra) and feel it circulating and penetrating your solar plexus. Many of us carry a lot of repressed emotion in this area of our bodies, which is tied to our will and sense of empowerment, the overall feeling of who we are. You may need to breathe several times to this area. Let the healing Earth energy gently open your belly and loosen those places that are tight, that are holding onto old energies and fears. When you feel relaxed and open, and you can feel a warmth here spreading, then you know you can move on.

On the fifth in-breath, breathe the energy up to your chest (fourth chakra) and feel it envelope and penetrate your heart. Feel it expand in your chest cavity, your lungs, your ribs. The heart area carries so much old emotion, and many of us have deep hurts here. Gently let Mother Earth touch this place in you. Do this breath as many times as you need until you feel warmth spreading, until you feel a relaxing and an opening of this area. Let whatever you have been holding be released back into the Earth, let it melt away and down through the soles of your feet back into the Earth. Just as a mother is not harmed by soothing and receiving her children's griefs and troubles, Mother Earth is never damaged by your connecting to her like this.

On the sixth in-breath, breathe the energy up to your throat (fifth chakra) and feel it opening this area, which is connected to your voice and speaking your truth. Then exhale it back down to the Earth.

On the seventh in-breath, breathe the energy up to the middle of

your forehead between your eyes (sixth chakra—third eye) and feel this part of you, connected to spiritual vision, higher perception and intuition, opening and being gently caressed, connected to Mother Earth. Exhale back down into the Earth.

On the eighth and final in-breath, bring the energy all the way up to the top of your head (7th chakra-crown) and feel the top of your head opening to spiritual guidance and to light from the cosmos. Feel Mother Earth's energy caressing and opening this area, grounding you between the Earth and sky, as a child of Earth and the cosmos. Fill your face, your skull, your brain, your glands, your hair, with this green nurturing light, connecting you to all of life. On your final exhale, breathe the energy out through your hands—down your arms and out through your palms and back into Mother Earth. This creates a complete circle of energy. Now you are connected to what is sustaining you in life, what is always there for you. This potent green life force energy can help you heal, revitalize, and balance your whole being.

Grounding and Cosmic Energy Meditation
(Hollis Polk)

Please sit comfortably someplace where you are well supported, with your feet flat on the floor and your hands resting comfortably and separately in your lap or on the arms of the chair.

Now… Please close your eyes, and take a deep breath. Breathe in really deeply, and as you let it out, just… relax… consciously letting go in your muscles and melting into whatever you are sitting on. Now… take another deep breath… and notice whatever you are sitting on holding you up, notice how easy and comfortable and solid that is… now take another deep breath in and as you let it out, notice the temperature of the air on your cheek and just let that … relax you… even more…

Take another deep breath in… and as you exhale, begin to focus on the base of your spine… And with the next deep breath in… and the next deep breath out… imagine that there's a small plug at the base of your spine… and just… gently… ease that out… and now imagine that there's a current of energy flowing down from the base of your spine… you may see

this energy as a cord, or a color, flowing down, or you may feel it as a texture or a temperature, or you may even hear it as a tone … flowing gently, easily and automatically… down from the base of your spine through whatever you're sitting on… down into the floor … and through the floor and the space below that, and whatever floor and spaces are beneath that … through the foundation of the building, and down into the dirt below that… and let it keep flowing down… down… down… through the dirt, into the bedrock beneath you… flowing down… through the bedrock, through the earth's crust, down into the earth's mantle… down… down… down… into the molten core of the earth… and allow anything in your body or any energy in or around you that needs to be healed or transformed to flow down your grounding cord into the earth, where Mother Earth can heal it and transform it.

And allow a bit of that healing, transforming energy to begin to rise up a cord, that is parallel to your grounding cord. … you may see this energy as a beam of light in a particular color, flowing up or you may feel it as a temperature or a texture, or you may even hear it as a tone… or a harmony… And allow this lovely energy to rise… up from the core of the earth, up through the earth's mantle, up into the earth's crust and through the earth's crust, up into the bedrock below your feet, up into the dirt, up into the foundation of the building, up through any space above that, up through the floor, up into the waiting open charkas of your feet.

The pad of each toe has a small chakra, like a vortex, which opens like the iris of a camera. And there's a larger chakra in the very center of each foot, which also opens like the iris of a camera. As the wonderful earth energy reaches your feet, it flows up, gently and easily, through the open foot charkas into your feet, swirling through them, healing and transforming, warming and soothing, filling them with this wonderful energy, wonderful light, or warmth or even texture or sound. And as it fills your feet, it swirls up through the ankle joints, warming and healing, soothing and transforming… letting go…

And this lovely color, or warmth, or tone or energy continues to flow on up… up… up into your calves, flowing along the bones, warming and relaxing, soothing and letting go and radiating out, out into the tendons, the muscles, the fascia, the skin, and even filling the energy field around your legs…

And the energy continues to flow up, swirling and healing up through your knees, warming, softening, letting go…

And the energy continues to move up along the bones of your thighs, warming and healing, softening and relaxing, loosening and letting go. It moves out from the bones, out into the tendons, the muscles, the fascia, the skin, and even filling the energy field around your thighs with this wonderful light or warmth or sound or energy. Just healing and soothing and relaxing… letting go…

And the energy continues to swirl and heal as it moves from your thighs up into your pelvic cradle. The energy pools and swirls, heals and transforms as it relaxes the muscles and all the internal organs. You may see this as light filling your pelvic cradle, or feel it as an energy or a warmth or a texture, or even hear a tone. And as this energy fills your pelvic cradle, you notice a small

81

trickle of this wonderful earth energy continue down your grounding cord, back down into the earth, completing a circuit. So you know you are a part of the earth's energy…

And with that still running, begin to focus your attention out in the center of the universe… and allow a wonderful colored light… or perhaps a tone… or a warmth… or texture… to begin to flow down from the center of the universe…

Down into the Milky Way galaxy…
Down into the solar system…
Down into earth's atmosphere…
Down into the sky above your head…
And down into the roof over
your head…

And down through the space under that, though any beams and ceilings and even floors, if there are any, into the space just above your head…

And down into the crown of your head… and from there to the base of your skull and down along the backs of your vertebrae… vertebra by vertebra… along your neck and down along the vertebrae at the back of your chest, and along your lumbar vertebrae to the base of your spine.

And a little bit of this energy flows from the base of your spine down along your grounding cord into the center of the earth. Now you know YOU are the connection of earth energy and cosmic energy, of Mother Earth and Father Sky. You may even feel a little tug at the base of your spine and the top of your head as you acknowledge this connection… or you may feel yourself automatically sit just a little bit straighter in your chair…

And more of this wonderful cosmic energy mixes into your pelvic cradle… you may see your pelvic cradle filled with both colors simultaneously, or see them blend to make yet a third color, or see one color shot through with sparkles of the other… however you see it is fine… you may feel an unusual feeling, or you may hear two tones or a harmony… and as this wonderful color or sound or feeling floods your pelvic cradle, it expands into your energy field around your lower torso and expands by flowing up the front channels of your spine, rising up… up… up… gently and easily to fill your heart center… and it expands from there to fill your chest and your shoulders and the energy begins to flow down your arms, filling your arms and flowing and swirling down… down through your elbows into your lower arms and down through them into your wrists... swirling through your wrists into your hands filling them with this lovely light or tone or feeling...just allow that to happen... and the energy drips out through your palms and fingers into the space around you, filling the space around your hands and your arms and your chest with this lovely color... or sound... or feeling.... And the energy begins to rise again—up from your shoulders into your head... filling your head with this wonderful feeling... or sound... or color... until the energy flows out the top of your head to a place 18 to 24 inches above your head where it becomes a fountain... the energy flows down around your entire energy field, cleansing it, healing it, warming it, relaxing it, filling it with this wonderful, healing light, or sound or feeling, cleansing it, clearing it... gently moving out anything which less than healthy for you...

And just enjoy that amazing feeling of being the connection of earth and sky, in you and around you...

And just enjoy that wonderful flow of energy...

And when you are ready... come back to the room... open your eyes... move around... you may want to lean over and touch the floor to let go of any excess energy...

being completely in your body

aware...

awake...

alive...

and

refreshed!

Grounding While Lying Down Meditation
(Hollis Polk)

You could use this meditation for those CE-5s where you are lying on a blanket under the stars.

Please lie on your back, supported comfortably by pillows, or whatever you need. You should be comfortably warm, but still cool enough that you stay awake…

Take a deep breath in… and as you exhale… just allow yourself to feel the support of whatever you're lying on… take another deep breath in, and as you exhale… just feel that support on your back… and on the backs of your legs… feel that support on your heels and on your arms.

Now… take another deep breath in… and as you exhale… feel the temperature of the air on your cheek… really notice it… is it warm… is it cool… is it just right… is the temperature of the air the same on both cheeks… allow yourself to gently notice this…

Now… take another deep breath in… and as you let it out, just notice how well your head is supported… and how relaxed you feel…

And as you relax, you can begin to notice how whatever you're lying on is a part of the earth. Whatever it is made from comes, in one way or another, from the earth, whether it's feathers that come from ducks that walked the earth and were fed by it or whether it is wood from trees that grew in the earth or even carpet made from oil from inside the earth… or something else entirely… and so you ARE lying on the earth. And you can imagine that you are lying directly on the earth… maybe you're lying on a pile of leaves or on the forest floor or in a field of grass or on a beach or some other wonderful natural place… you are lying on the earth…

And you can begin to allow your muscles to just melt into the earth… let your arms melt … let your legs melt… let your ribcage melt… just feel them sinking into the earth… and you can imagine their energy flowing down through the dirt beneath you … down into the bedrock… down through the bedrock into the earths mantle… flowing down through the earth's mantle quickly and easily… down into the molten core of the earth.

Now imagine that this flow of energy is a giant cord, a giant grounding cord, connecting every cell in your body to the very center of the earth. And now imagine that Mother Earth is sending you her love, as energy, up this grounding cord. You may see this energy as… a beam of light in a particular color, flowing up… or you may feel it as a temperature or a texture, or you may even hear it as a tone… or a harmony… And allow this lovely energy to rise… up from the core of the earth, up through the earth's mantle, up into the earth's crust and through the earth's crust, up into the bedrock below you, up into the dirt, up into your waiting cells. And each and every one of your cells soaks up Mother Earth's love and

knows it is connected to Mother Earth. And each cell is renewed and refreshed by its connection to Mother Earth.

Mother Earth wants you to have lots of energy. So as you come back to normal, waking awareness, you begin to move around, easily and gently. Perhaps you move your fingers and toes, and now your hands and feet. And now your legs and arms and even your head and torso. You feel…

aware…

awake…

alive…

refreshed…

and ready to go!

REMOTE VIEWING

Remote Viewing is recommended as a viable method to communicate with ET by astronaut Dr. Edgar Mitchell. Dr. Mitchell created the organization The Foundation for Research Into Extraterrestrial and Extraordinary Encounters (FREE). One of our longest standing group members, Keiko, is our resident student of remote viewing. Here is what she has to share:

RV (Remote Viewing) is a practice that helps us to develop our innate ability to see and sense particular locations, physical structures, persons, events, without needing to physically be there to see or sense them. Remote Viewing is about viewing, hearing, smelling, tasting, feeling sensations, and feeling emotions in remote time and space. You may have randomly experienced similar paranormal phenomenon such as déjà vu or premonitions. In contrast, RV is consciously done by focusing on an 'objective' while you are in the meditative state.

How to Remote View

- Sit quietly and let go of your busy mind and empty yourself.
- Connect yourself to an objective and know you are connected.
- Describe and draw information that you receive through your five senses and more, as raw information. In other words, describe the information without making up your own stories. (Synchronizing the right and left hemispheres of brain.) You are trying to get away from imagination, memory and/or deduction.
- Organize and analyze information.

Abilities/Attitudes You Can Develop by Remote Viewing

By synchronizing the right and left hemispheres of the brain during RV practice we can develop our psychic abilities. As well, sensing remote objectives gives us the experience of oneness. Realizing that we are connected to each other with our thoughts/intentions can make us humble to others.

An experienced trainer of RV at the Monroe Institute has said that he has never encountered any individual who could not view or sense anything at the end of a one-weekend workshop. We all have the ability and can develop the ability by practicing. The practice will give you confirmation of your true nature of being non-local and one with the unified field of consciousness.

To Start Practicing Remote Viewing

In his DVDs, Dr. Greer recommends sharpening our intuition by practicing with these exercises:

- Sense who the caller is before picking up the phone
- Sense who visitor is before opening the door
- Sense an object which someone has placed in a box a photo or words placed in an envelope

There are different methods and techniques of Remote Viewing to choose from. You can find books, DVDs, workshops, website, etc. on RV. There are apps and websites offering RV objectives such as http://www.rvtargets.com/. It's free of charge to register and use it.

How to Use Remote Viewing for CE-5

When in the field during CE-5, start by meditating with a mantra, sound, visualization, guided meditation etc. When you reach the quiet state, begin focusing on your objective:

- Vector ET to your location by going into space, and then returning to your location with your awareness
- Visit a planet, galaxy, star
- Encounter different galactic civilizations
- Meet a Star Being
- Go to the International Space Station
- Go to a Galactic Meeting
- Go to the Space Station on the Rings of Saturn

As it was mentioned previously, Remote Viewing is not just about picking up the sights, sounds, textures and smells of a location. You can also pick up the emotions, feelings, and thoughts that a place offers. Some astronauts had the following feelings and thoughts while they were floating in space:

- Everybody is connected to each other
- It's a familiar place, like home
- There is no absolute
- We need to take care of each other

What will you see/feel when remote viewing in space while your body is in a circle at the contact site?

Links
Learn more about Remote Viewing at the links below.

Prudence Calabrese's Remote Viewing Course (7 videos) https://youtu.be/uij1clj9FzY
The Secret History of US Remote Viewing https://youtu.be/kUOu7MJnpO4
Ingo Swan – Human Super Sensitivities and the Future https://youtu.be/rHH5PBS2H_I
Dr. Hal Puthoff on Remote Viewing https://youtu.be/FOAfH1utUSM
Joe McMoneagle, The Stargate Chronicles, MUFON Conv 2/16/06 https://youtu.be/egk7V8XKRWQ
John Vivanco Psychic Spy – Part 1 of 3 https://youtu.be/ZTEtvMoUjas
John Vivanco Psychic Spy – Part 2 of 3 https://youtu.be/y0W8MHbZ9N0
John Vivanco Psychic Spy – Part 3 of 3 https://youtu.be/NXvT0OC98Nc
Lessons Learned from the Stargate Program with Edwin May https://youtu.be/L811nO601sg

BIO-ELECTROMAGNETIC COMMUNICATION

Humans have the potential to emit a very powerful force field. I've had an accidental moment of telekinesis, which evidences this for myself. We believe that this section is the leading edge of CE-5 and our own evolution. Many thanks to Jeremy of CE-5 Aotearoa in New Zealand, who shared with us this advanced technique of communication.

This process is specifically focused on energetic communication through the bio-electromagnetic field of the heart: the torus. It is based within experiential learning from several cases of verified close proximity contact and interaction.

Principles:

• The geometric shape used to describe the self-reflexive nature of consciousness is the torus. The torus can be used to define the workings of consciousness itself; therefore, consciousness has geometry.

• The torus allows a vortex of energy to form, bending back along itself and re-entering itself. It 'inside-outs', continuously flowing back into itself. Therefore, toroidal energy is continually refreshing itself and continually influencing itself.

• When the torus is in balance and the energy is flowing we are in the perfect state to be our authentic selves. Authenticity is a key component in connecting to ET and celestial beings.

• The heart's magnetic field is toroidal and communicates throughout the body and into the external environment. It is a non-verbal energetic communication modality that can be used to communicate effectively with each other, the environment and other types of beings.

• Because electromagnetic toroidal fields are holographic, it is likely that the sum total of our Universe is present within the frequency spectrum of a single torus. This means each one of us is connected to the entire Universe and can access all the information within it at any given moment.

Process Outline:

This is an outline of the general process that should be formed into a guided meditation and delivered by the team facilitator. This process in not fixed, it is a 'work in progress' and should be approached with creativity and flexibility. Significant contact events can occur during this process; therefore, adaptability is often necessary. Be guided within what naturally occurs and stay present within the coherent energy and the above principles.

• Focus on working as a completely unified CE-5 team with the shared collective intent of Universal peace and oneness. Specific teams can be formed with those who naturally resonate with this intention.

• Establish a coherent toroidal energy field within the CE-5 team. If it is the first time doing this process, complete the Resonant Energy Meditation first. Once familiar with establishing a coherent toroidal energy field, create it in your own way that works best for your team, then continue with this process. Put new ideas to the test.

• Consciously choose to bind the shared collective intent of the team within the structure of the toroidal energy field. Focus on being one. Merge your heart based divine will into the toroidal form and enliven the full colour spectrum, seeing the form more clearly and brightly in consciousness, notice how it surrounds you. Consciously merge it with others in the team.

• E-motion, energy in motion. Energize the toroidal field by filling your heart centre with the emotions of love, joy, peace, gratitude, etc. Allow these feelings to overflow and merge within the vibratory structure of the torus, feeling an increase in the rate of energy flow and seeing it activate further as a result. Focus on a singluar zero point heart energy within the centre of the circle, this being the heart centre of the team.

• Acknowledge that each one of us is connected to the entire Universe and can access all the information within it at any given moment, through our heart centre. When we access what is present in our hearts, we are literally connecting to the limitless supply and wisdom of the Universe. This enables what we refer to as miracles to be present with us. Embrace this knowing that exists within our heart centre. Allow it to simply resonate as Universal Truth and radiate from our being.

• Hold this space open for communication. Transmit energetic information through the electromagnetic toroidal spectrum of the heart. Initially, focus on an energetic invitation. Transmit this invitation into the immediate environment and then into the distant surroundings by expanding the toroidal form in consciousness. Scale it up to embrace the entire planet, then scale it down to the local area. Repeat several times expanding further each time, right out into space, continually inviting all beings who resonate with the intent. Move effortlessly in consciousness through the toroidal connectivity. Know that the information you communicate through this form is likely to be received by other sentient beings. Radiate the energy of invitation and what you believe to be of shared importance in establishing communication. Make sure to also hold space for responses.

• Fluctuate your focus within all parameters of the shared toroid, expanding the toroidal awareness by seeing it as infinitely large and infinitely small at the same time, both internally and externally. Consciously follow heart centred magnetic attractions to certain locations, initially within the local environment, then in other parameters. Resonate the intention to connect with the beings that could be there in that specific location. Allow yourself to fully expand and feel as much as you can. Ask them to verify their presence in ways that are obvious and undoubtedly true for you and the team. If communication is verified, guide the team to focus the heart centred energy on that specific parameter and ask the beings to be as present and interactive as they are able to. Hold the energy for them to connect further and enjoy the love of being an ambassador of Earth.

MUSIC AND SOUND

Barbara Marciniak talks about the importance of sound among her collection of channelling:

"Sound is a tool for transformation. Keepers of frequency, which we are encouraging you to become, learn how to modulate the frequency they hold through sound. Sound can penetrate any substance, move molecules, and re-arrange realities. You can begin to work with sound by allowing it to play your body. Get yourself centered, clear your mind, and allow tones to come through you. The ancient mystery schools worked with sound in this manner, and it is a very powerful technique when done in a group. You will go very far with your use of sound after working with it for awhile. It is like a powerful tool being given to an infant. Without proper awareness, you could do things, and not realize the ramifications of what you're doing.

"Think about what sound does in stadiums and auditoriums. The cheering or booing of a crowd creates an ambiance. When groups of you make sound together, you create an ambiance for yourselves. You allow certain energies to play the instruments of your bodies. You let go of pre-conceived ideas, and allow different melodies and energies to use your physical bodies as opportunities to represent themselves on the planet. In actuality, what you experience is the life force of energies that you allow to express through your own selves. You become channels. You allow a vibration to come onto the planet in its full glory through your bodies and your joint cooperation. You birth something. You create an opportunity and energy takes advantage of that opportunity.

"Sound is going to evolve. Now human beings can become instruments for sound through toning. Certain combinations of sounds played through the body unlock information and frequencies of intelligence. Being silent for a long period after the harmonics allows human beings to use their bodies as devices to receive and absorb the frequencies, and to use the vehicle of breathing to take them into an ecstatic state. When you tone with others, you have access to the group mind that you did not have prior to making the sound. The key word is "harmony."

"What you intend to do with sound is of utmost importance. If you are not clear about your intentions, sound can have a way of enveloping on itself, and outgrowing its original capacity. It doubles and quadruples itself with its own impact. It is very important for you to have a clear intention of what you plan on doing with sound. Sound stirs energy up. It creates a standing columnar wave, building frequency upon frequency. This energy can then be directed at, or toward anything. When you make sound in a circle, or in the circumference of the pillar of light, you create a column that is capable of many more things that you ever realized. It is capable of creating explosions, and of destroying and creating many realities."

From *Bringers of The Dawn*
https://www.pleiadians.com/dawn.html

Using Sound in CE-5

Music is a powerful tool. It moves us, changes us, and uplifts us. Sound can support our ability to relax and turn inward and makes it easier to connect to universal one.

During CE-5 you can:

- Play sounds/songs in the background of group chatting, instruction or meditating

- Play sounds/songs as a focus of the group

- Sing together

- Chant together

- Do a Puja

- Hum

- Tone

- Drum

- Didgeridoo it up

- Use singing bowls

- Ring bells

- Hit tuning forks

- Etc.

Do what calls to you and supplement your CE-5 agenda with whatever the group likes best.

If you are interested in sound as a healing tool for yourself, you could:

- Go to Tom Kenyon's sound healing page: http://tomkenyon.com/music-sound-healing

- Listen to Mozart, or anything else that uplifts you. Samoiya Shelley Yates talks about this in her amazing story: https://www.youtube.com/watch?v=KHGyu_AXNWg&t=9s

- Go to the Monroe Institute to get some hemi-sync CDs: https://www.monroeinstitute.org/store

- Grab the Omnec Onec Soul Journey meditation which is a beautiful symphony flowing through all states of consciousness: http://omnec-onec.com/meditation-cdsouljourney/

- Listen to the first three minutes of Beethoven's 7th symphony. According to Bashar, this music has a profound healing effect: https://www.youtube.com/watch?v=RpJeWvFZ_fg&t=1675s

PUJAS

A puja is a ceremony that originated in India and honours and worships Hindu deities. It is often ritualized with accoutrements such as a large thali (tray), candles, bell, brass or silver cups/bowls and spoons, pure water, sage, incense sticks, flowers, fruit, uncooked rice, and images and/or figurines of the Ascended Masters.

A Puja is sung in the Sanskrit language. Sanskrit is thought to be the root of all Indo-European languages. It is ancient: it may be the remnant of a language spoken during the last Golden Age and its origin may be interstellar. Sanskrit words are thought to be the most precise sound intonation that most accurately matches that which the word describes. If used correctly with high states of consciousness some believe that one can manifest using the Sanskrit language.

In the context of CE-5, the puja is secularized. Instead, the ceremony represents not a prayer to a particular deity but a general prayer, worship, or honouring of the cosmos or to the collective lineage of Ascended Masters (e.g. such as Buddha, Babaji, Krishna, Jesus, Sai Baba, etc.), who have assisted and still assist in the spiritual development of our world. Doing a puja during a CE-5 can be very simple. Set up some crystals or other sacred objects on a small table, burn a candle and light incense. Sage is also good to burn. Chant "Om" several times and then sing the Puja for a little while. Let the candle and incense burn until the CE-5 is done.

Pujas to Include in a CE-5:

Isha Yoga Guru Pooja
Dr. Greer sings a very long, involved puja. It would take a very long time to memorize it, so the easy thing to do is to find it on YouTube and convert it to mp3 with an online YouTube to mp3 converter (like https://ytmp3.com/). Search: "Joshua Tree 2015 - Puja with Dr. Steven Greer" https://www.youtube.com/watch?v=iN2dpW2mjn0

Im Nah Mah
This mantra translates to "close to God" or "one with the higher being." The melody of this is: G-C-C (or any other fifth interval). Once you sing the melody a few times for people to catch the tune, have everyone continue the chant internally for the duration of the meditation.

To hear what it sounds like, you can find it on YouTube if you search for "Cosmic Consciousness Meditation Part 1 of 5" (https://www.youtube.com/watch?v=vo72V0S2me8)

Gayatri Mantra

This mantra adores the goddess Gayatri, who is not considered a deity or demigod, but the single supreme personality. A lovely, upbeat puja that celebrates our movement into the feminine as Goddess energy swells and gains momentum during this transformative time. Search "Gayatri Mantra" on YouTube to hear the tune. There are several versions; pick your favourite melody.

Om bhoor bhuvah svah
Tat savitur varenyam
Bhargo devasya dhimahi
Dhiyo yo nah prachodayat

Translation:
(Oh) Supreme one; (who is) the physical, astral (and) causal worlds (herself).
 (you are) the source of all, deserving all worship
 (O) Radiant, divine one; (we) meditate (upon you)
Propel our Intellect (towards liberation or freedom)

Moola Mantra

This mantra evokes the living God, asking for protection and freedom from all sorrow and suffering. Search "Moola Mantra" on YouTube to hear versions of the tune.

Om
Sat Chit Ananda Parabrahma
Purushothama Paramatma
Sri Bhagavathi Sametha
Sri Bhagavathe Namaha

Translation:
Om: We are calling on the highest energy, of all there is
Sat: The formless
Chit: Consciousness of the universe
Ananda: Pure love, bliss and joy
Para brahma: The supreme creator
Purushothama: Who has incarnated in human form to help guide mankind
Paramatma: Who comes to me in my heart, and becomes my inner voice
Sri Bhagavati: The divine mother, the power aspect of creation
Same tha: Together with
Sri Bhagavate: The Father of creation, which is unchangeable and permanent
Namaha: I thank you and acknowledge this presence in my life

The Pushpak Aircraft by Balasaheb Pandit Pant Pratinidhi, 1916

TONING AND HUMMING

Keiko is also our experienced sound worker. Here is what she has to say about toning and humming:

Our own voice can be a tool that promotes healing and transformation at all levels of our existence. Toning is a great tool for emotional enhancement and clearance. It can be relaxing and uplifting at the same time. Humming can be calming and can take you to a deep meditative state.

When we tone or hum, the vocalization process stimulates our brains, and the sound vibration goes through the whole inside of our bodies even before we hear the sound. When we hear the sound, it further stimulates the brain and vibrates the entire outer body. All this moves us at molecular levels to bring us back to a natural and balanced state.

Sound is also a carrier of information. When we have a desired outcome, we can use sound with intention. It is a powerful way to manifest, and it is easy and effective. Transformation will happen when you recognize its power within and without you. Just as when you tone with over one hundred people, although you cannot discern your own voice, you know that you are a part of the grand harmony.

Toning or Humming in a group raises coherency, amplifies energy and intensifies intentions. When we tone or hum with loving thoughts and appreciation, we can create a powerful vibrational field of love, and can thus bring light to the planet.

Toning and humming are also ways to communicate in higher vibrational dimensions. In our own dimension we can use toning and humming to communicate with our babies, animals, plants and of course, star beings.

How to Tone: Usually elongated vowel sounds are used for toning, such as AH (as in "ma"), EEE (as in "me"), OOO (as in "you"), OH (as in "go"), etc. Often the sound AH is used to tone because it is associated with our heart chakras and has a powerful energy. It is also said in Buddhist teachings that AH is the original sound of creation and by singing AH we can be one with universal energy. OM, which is the well-known primordial sound of creation (in Hindu tradition), is sounded AUM (AH-OOO-M).

   1. Relax.
   2. Set your intention.
   3. Sing with a vowel sound with one full breath. Repeat. You can tone at any pitch, loudness, or quality that you are comfortable and resonate with. However, listen to yourself and others to be harmonious as well. If your vocal codes are stressed, then hum a while to ease the stress.
   4. After a minimum of 5 - 10 minutes of toning, be silent to maximize the effect of the toning.

How to Hum: Humming is the simplest way to produce the most effective self-created sound. It is also said that humming is the sound of creation and it is always within us. So we are always humming, conscious of it or not.

   1. Relax. Set your intention.
   3. Close your lips and keep your upper teeth and lower teeth slightly apart.
   4. Project the sound into the oral cavity, nasal cavity, and the rest of the skull and chest cave.
   5. After a minimum of 5 minutes of humming, be silent to maximize the effect of humming.

OTHER SOUND STUFF

C#
The earth's orbit around the sun creates a hum so low it cannot be heard by the human ear. According to Bashar, an ET that channels through Darryl Anka, the frequency of this tone is approximately the same as the note C# (sharp) on our musical scale. Although the earth's musical path around the sun is 33 octaves lower than middle C on our pianos, you can still benefit from listening to this frequency in the range we can hear. Bashar says that if you immerse yourself in this tone you will find clarity and things will become more effortless. You will literally begin to "See Sharp." The earth will support you as it supports everything in nature. You could play this tone in the background while you are meditating on a CE-5. Several versions exist on YouTube:

C# solo: https://www.youtube.com/watch?v=6Q3KsrB1KM4
C# with melodic overtones and binaural beats:
https://www.youtube.com/watch?v=SBMXxm9X3P4&t=1254s
Bashar explains C#: https://www.youtube.com/watch?v=3v4pXOh6SKo

Anael and Bradfield
Anael and Bradfield are musicians who collaborated on the Fire the Grid project that Samoiya Shelley Yates spearheaded. (Her story is amazing and involves ET beings—search "Shelley Yates Vancouver Speech" on YouTube to hear her story.) *Sky Sent* and *Be Still Thy Soul* are two beautiful songs that are themed around ET disclosure and the shift that is happening now. I know of one CE-5 group that says that ET really seems to like it when they play the song *Sky Sent*. Listen to the lyrics and you'll understand why! Available on iTunes, or go to https://anael.net/.

Fun Songs Related to UFOs or ET:
Make a playlist for the road trip that gets you to that special remote location:

- Anael and Bradfield - *Sky Sent*
- Babes in Toyland - *Calling Occupants of Interplanetary Craft* (Cover)
- Billy Bragg - *My Flying Saucer*
- Billy Thorpe - *Children of the Sun*
- Blue Rodeo - *Cynthia*
- The Carpenters - *Calling Occupants of Interplanetary Craft* (Cover)
- Credence Clearwater Revival - *It Came Out of the Sky*
- David Bowie - *Starman*
- Elton John - *I've Seen The Saucers*
- Five Man Electrical Band - *I'm A Stranger Here*
- Husker Du - *Books About UFOs*
- Jefferson Airplane - *Have You Seen The Saucers?*
- Kesha - *Spaceship* (Kesha saw several UFOs in Joshua Tree in 2017)
- Klaatu - *Calling Occupants of Interplanetary Craft* (Inspired by World Contact Day)
- Spiritualized - *Ladies & Gentlemen, We are Floating In Space*
- Yes - *Arriving UFO*

SAMPLE CE-5 AGENDAS

Model your first few CE-5s after one of the following agendas, until you develop your own unique style:

Our Typical CE-5
- To prepare, meditate three times in the week previous to fieldwork
- On the day of contact, sit in a circle and set the group intention
- Tone the word "Om" together three times as an opening
- Do an eyes closed meditation to connect to one mind consciousness
- Orientate everyone to the constellations, planets, north star etc.
- Do another meditation, eyes open, watching the sky
- Sky watch and trade stories, laugh, eat snacks, get cozy in sleeping bags
- To close, thank everyone and ET

CE-5 for Science Folks
- Sit in a circle and set intentions for the night
- Do an orientation of the sky
- Review essential elements of contact: one mind connection, a sincere heart, clear intention
- Play a Dr. Greer meditation about Coherent Thought Sequencing
- Let an astronomy expert teach about constellations, stars, planets etc.
- Sky watch and teach how to discern what is a verified UFO is or isn't
- Review the most legitimate UFO encounters, officially released documents, etc.
- Discuss interplay between spirituality and science, emotions and logic, heart and mind
- Silent sky watch disconnected from analysis/thinking… instead, focus on oneness, and/or love
- Close with thanks and appreciation for each other's participation in this experiment

CE-5 for Spiritual Folks
- Sit in a circle, hold hands, and do an opening prayer
- Set an intention for the night
- Do a clearing meditation
- Have someone lead a oneness meditation
- Have some silent sky watching time
- Sing a Puja together, or have one person sing it
- Do a meditation to receive channelled messages sent to the group
- Play some singing bowls or the didgeridoo
- More sky watch
- Closing: Hold hands, bless and thank Mother Earth, Father Sky, each other, Source, and ET

Matt Maribona's CE-5
- Go outside
- Think about all the times in your life that you have felt love, such as when you fell in love, held a baby, witnessed the passing of a loved one, enjoyed an ice cream on a summer day, had a puppy lick your face, watched a sunset, smiled at a stranger, danced to great music, felt the harmony of nature, etc.
- Look up, knowing ET is out there, and say "Hi"

Josh's K.I.S.S. CE-5
- Listen to a Dr. Greer meditation
- Play Pink Floyd and watch the sky

CE-5 Modelled off of a CSETI Training Expedition with Dr. Greer
- Before the start, play crop circle tones on speakers. Use a walkie-talkie or radio transmitter to broadcast the tones out into space. Do this while setting up and during breaks.
- General discussion, question and answer period.
- Do a sky orientation.
- Use laser pointers to signal to ET the location of the team.
- The puja ceremony begins when there is some kind of signal like an anomalous light. Stand for the ceremony. Alternatively, a few words of gratitude that we have found each other and are willing to meet for the purpose of bringing cosmic peace to our planet.
- Lead into a meditation and then sit silently in meditation for 30 to 45 minutes. Assign one person as the sky watcher while the group closes eyes during this meditation.
- Debrief from meditation and discussion for about an hour while observing any ET events.
- Have break for snacks, social conversation and bio breaks.
- Do another round of meditation, followed by debriefing and discussion.
- Close circle by holding hands and generating a feeling of gratitude.
- Post fieldwork conviviality with wine, cheese and crackers.

Lyssa Royal Holt's CE-5
- Do an opening ceremony including sage, welcoming the local spirits and guides of the land.
- Ask permission for presence on the land using a mantra such as the Gayatri Mantra.
- Lyssa does a channelling on the topic of the day's learning—if you do not have a channeller, pick a topic for development and speak to it. At Lyssa's events, the beings continue via channelling to lead the group through a contact meditation.
- If strange phenomena such as weather anomalies occur, work with that to view what is happening beyond human perception that often translates through the environment.
- Work with a photo of ET to connect with the being's energy.
- The agenda is fluid and depends on circumstances, conditions, the group, and the messages.

CE-5 Aotearoa – CE-5 for New People
- Plan an informal meeting to discuss the CE-5 prior to field trip.
- If choosing a new location, ask ET for guidance and ask them to confirm it with an obvious sign.
- Invite anyone who wishes to learn about CE-5, within the agreement of what is required as a team.
- Practice Coherent Thought Sequencing (through the CSETI app) prior to the event.
- At the event: Welcome by event facilitator, introductions, site/sky orientation, what to expect, etc.
- Buddy system: pair new people with experienced whenever possible.
- Individuals share their intention for being at the event.
- Open with a ceremony calling on all to assist with our transition into peace to join with us. Extend gratitude and give thanks to them and each other.
- Fill your heart with love by acknowledging all you are grateful for, each other, family, partner, pets, the Earth, being able to do CE-5, etc.
- CTS opening meditation, then in to silent meditation (cont'd on next page)

- Group sharing then a short break and walk over site for those who wish to do so, experienced people supporting those new to CE-5.
- Meditations and discussion/sharing for the rest of the evening, going with what naturally occurs.
- Close with a gratitude ceremony, thanks, prayers, music, etc.

CE-5 Aotearoa – CE-5 for Experienced Teams

- Plan an event for 3 or 4 nights. More time often allows for deeper experiences.
- Do daily Coherent Thought Sequencing (CTS) meditations for this site at least two weeks prior.
- Set the intention to connect further with specific beings that contact has been established with. Communicate clearly in CTS that you would like the relationship to be mutually beneficial.
- Get to know each other and bond as it helps form a coherent team. The closer we are the closer they are. Picture each other's faces (including non-humans) when doing CTS and focus on working as one.
- Create an email list for those attending the event and encourage communication.
- Write down any dreams, Out of Body Experiences (OBEs), RV, numeric sequences or other experiences that might be related to the event. Share with everyone on the email list.
- Eat light foods (preferably vegetarian) a week before and during the event.
- Start with an opening prayer/toning and then group sharing.
- Progress with a resonant energy meditation or similar to align the energy centres of everyone in the team. Anchor this to the Earth then extend out and within to all parameters.
- Hold the energetic space of love, joy, gratitude and peace within the team centre.
- Hold the intention for beings to 'merge' with the team.
- Go through the bio-electromagnetic communication process, then into silent meditation, then into 'speak what you see.' Speak what you see sessions are when the team is in a shared state of RV (ideally) and can therefore access parts of the same information. Ask for confirmation through technology present (tri-field meters etc.) and/or through shared collective experience (images, feelings, unusual sensations, attraction to certain areas on the site, etc.).
- If there are meter responses to information progress to a Q&A session: clarify who you are in contact with "Can you please confirm we are in contact with an ET being" etc., asking the being types to confirm (ET, Celestial, Spirit etc.). If using a meter, ask questions with a "Yes" or "No" answer; "No" can often be silence, however make sure you clarify what "Yes" is. If there are shared images or feelings etc., stay focused on them and develop them further, energetically asking for more information/understanding. Ask beings present to merge with the team. Go with the flow.
- Focus on energy flow and information 'downloads.'
- If an energetic 'lock-on' occurs (usually measured with a tri-field meter) the team can hold hands and put their feet on the ground so the energy is distributed and anchored. Distribute the energy freely among CE-5 teams all over the world, simply by having the intention to do so. Keep the intensity of these downloads light by holding the feeling of joy and anchoring it to the Earth. Smile. ☺ Allow information to become known.
- Meditations and discussion/sharing for the rest of the evening, going with what naturally occurs. Encourage the team to be freely sharing everything that is experienced.
- Close with a gratitude ceremony for all those who attended.

Robert Bingham's Instructions for How to Summon UFOs

- Start with an open heart and an open mind. Have a good intention. Concentrate on a spot in the sky. Telepathically say: "Please Come. Thank you." Observe the sky.

CE-5 Activities During a Kosta ETLet'sTalk Retreat:
- Do an opening meditation connecting the group to each other, to the Global CE-5 Community, and to The Universal One.
- Do an energy clearing meditation so that only positive energies comprise the group field.
- Orient and teach about constellations, stars and planets in the night sky.
- Teach proper identification of ET versus man-made craft and natural sky and ground phenomena.
- Teach proper protocol for sightings involving sky locations, use of pointing devices, etc.
- Conduct sky watch and meditate. (For sky watches, alternate between silent sky watch and sky watch where talk is allowed.)
- Share significant stories of ET Contact at appropriate times throughout the night.
- Break for bio needs, snacks and socializing.
- Do more meditation alternating with sky watch.
- Close out the fieldwork by holding hands and thanking everyone there including ET.

James Gilliland's ET Contact

James does not run an agenda. The sky watch that happens at the ECETI ranch is casual and fun. As James says, "It's the land. They're just here." James' main tip to increase sightings: "To make contact, get your shit together." That means working on healing your shame, wounds, criticism, selfishness, attachment, greed, ego, etc. At the ranch, the main theme is joy. Cultivate your "Bliss Hits," welcome laughter and love, and put your eyes to the skies.

Alien Protocol's Advanced Protocol

Set aside one or two weeks of preparatory time where you:
- Do not eat meat or eggs.
- Do not partake in drugs or alcohol (medicine and ceremonial wine is ok).
- Sit down for two thirty minute meditations a day connecting to oneness and the universe, understanding your full nature, showing your exact location and visualizing a specific request of the encounter you wish to have.
- Have two ritual showers for five days to remove bad energy and raise vibration.
- Face your fears three times by meditating in a dark or creepy place... confront your fear with love.
- Increase theta brain waves with chocolate, mugwort tea, strategy/word games, and listening to binaural beats.

Fieldwork is done over at least two days, at a safe and private location:
- Cleanse the location with sage or sacred tobacco burn.
- As a group, meditate three times during the day and include Tai Chi/Solar Salutations, and toning/humming.
- At night, do meditations, vocal exercises, play harmonic sounds and connect to all.
- Include pen and paper for people to write requests, affirmations, prayers, feelings, remote viewing impressions.
- There are more protocols... the Alien Protocols Group says: "...if you've gotten this far you'll & they'll figure out the rest...wink wink!"

Sixto Paz Well's Advice

While we don't know how a Rahma contact event generally goes, we do have instructions from Sixto describing what he believes is one of the most important abilities to develop when contacting ETs. See "Channelling as a Group" in the Meditations section.

TROUBLESHOOTING

Not Up to Speed:

If you are for the most part depressed, anxious, resentful, cynical, skeptical in a hostile way (moderate skepticism is a good thing!), angry, entitled, mean, pessimistic, etc.... yes, you will still have consistent sightings... one day! For now you have some work to do to:

- Find a good counsellor or psychic, or find some self-help books, videos, or resources.

- Accept that you are responsible for your life and that you create your own reality and future, even if you have been dealt a crappy hand. Yes, life can sometimes suck, you could blame everyone else, and you may be justified, but where will that get you? Mobilize yourself and get in a better gear. Make peace with yourself and where you are.

Fears:

Our biggest collective fear about contact with ET may not be about abductions or Hollywood's portrayal of alien attacks. It may be the subconscious fear of losing our ego as we accelerate our vibration high enough to communicate with ET (see: Lyssa Royal Holt's book *Prepare for Contact*). If you give credence to channelled sources, you can rest easy, since many major sources state that you will not lose your individuality as you ascend, even when you ultimately reunify with Source. (Seth, Billy Fingers, The Hathors). Regardless of what you think your fears are, the more you do CE-5 and the more you relax and put your focus on what you want, and not focus on your fears, those fears will diminish with time and you will get the experiences you want.

And Now a Very Common CE-5 Discussion:

"Do negative ETs exist?"
There is some debate about this in the CE-5 world. This document is not meant to give you answers, it is meant to put you in the direction of your own exploration and discernment. Some think that any ET with the capability and technology to cross time and space is also inherently spiritually advanced. Some think that "service to self" races are or were here and have caused trouble.

Getting over differences in opinion is a big step in your evolutionary process. As you decide what it is that you believe, take care not to step on anyone else's beliefs. People come to their own conclusions for justified reasons. Each person is unique, with their own personalities, histories, triggers, fears, desires, previous belief systems, and realities. Yes, yes, you're probably right. And if you are indeed right, and you want to flaunt that badge of spiritual integrity beside your "I AM RIGHT" button, you must relax and allow others to operate from their own reality. (Wait a second, was that a spiritual ego trap?) Ultimate reality doesn't have much to do with solid, immutable facts. Each person is their own universe, and the essence of their lives lies more in their perspective and attitude than their words or material creations. To recap simply: if you think someone else is "wrong for being wrong" you're... wrong. Dang!

Regardless of whether you think Negative ETs exist, we can assure you that CE-5 is a safe place to be. **We have not heard of a single negative experience with an ET that has resulted from a CE-5.** "We" is a large number. Dozens of people have contributed to this handbook, with decades of combined experience in a network of thousands. If it happened, we would have heard about it. CE-5 people love to talk. (Certainly, there have been stories told by CE-5 folks having had negative experiences with... other CE-5 people!) Back to the topic, we believe that it is the loving heart space that must be cultivated to enter into this work that excludes negative ETs... if they exist.

"Okay, so, let's just be clear here. Is there any chance that I am going be abducted?"
Not if you are using any type of CE-5 protocol. Outside of CE-5, you have less to worry about now than in previous years. Abduction reports have declined.

Let's take a side trip and quickly go over what abductions might be, since it's a popular area of concern. Some believe that ETs participating in abductions were benevolent scientists, doing work with our DNA to protect our lineage and the process was not meant to scare us. They think that those of us who have gone through an abduction and were able to retain memories remember the event much like a child would remember having a medical procedure done that was against his or her will but beneficial in the long run. Others believe that the abductions were an uncompassionate project, where human DNA was harvested for the hybridization of an alien species or for other self-serving purposes. Regardless of which camp you are in, it's now thought by most everyone that any abductions that are happening in this day and age are military-industrial-complex-theatre, meant to scare the public and vilify all ETs. But, even in this case, when was the last time you heard about an abduction? Maybe the military's budget to freak us out is shrinking. Whatever they were, the heyday of abductions is over.

"So I don't need to be worried? I'm still worried. Convince me."
Well, maybe you should be a little cautious about negative entities.

"Did you just say negative entities? WTF!?"
Don't alarm yourself. What is a negative entity? If this subset of life exists, a negative entity could include: ghosts, spirits, inter-dimensionals, negative thought forms, a bad vibe, etc. That may sound scary, but if you are a good person and you generally feel well much of the time, you're covered. I explored this topic with a trusted channeller. Her guides said that these days negative entities are for the most part relatively harmless, because humanity has moved up the vibratory scale. In days long past, "demonic" possessions and disturbing effects from negative entities were more common. Negative entities are drawn to us because we are a powerful physical force that can balance them, and help them move out of their helpless inertia. They are parasitic more than anything else, and draw on our energy. She said they are plentiful, and to remember that our surroundings are also brimming with positive entities too. If you are vibrating high, you won't even notice these nuisances. If you would like to knock a few attached entities off you, sage or sweetgrass is every effective because of the smoke's dense, neutralizing properties. Or, do a clearing like the one James Gilliland has provided in the meditation section. Be sure to understand the subtle difference between the semantics of "protecting" yourself versus "healing/clearing." One positions you as a victim. The other positions you as a victor. Negative entities are only as powerful as you let them be. How do you know if you might have attracted one of these frivolous irritants? You can tell by the way you feel and by your behaviour. Even if you don't believe in negative entities, if you are being a jerk and you feel like crap, or you feel really sad, scared or tired, you should maybe do something about that!

"I'm stuck on the negative ET thing"

No problem, we have many in our group that believe that negative ETs exist, so we have thoroughly explored this area of concern. Let's soothe you with these theories:

- Some origin stories and channellings suggest that the process of disclosure is one of the ways that planets evolve. You may be part of a spiritual crew that goes from dark planet to dark planet, uplifting those that live under tyranny by helping them make contact with other civilizations from outer space. CE-5 and disclosure may be a sacred process of planetary upliftment that has universal backing and cannot be toyed with by malicious beings.

- In accordance with the "CE-5 is sacred" theory, it is very likely that a galactic federation made up of representatives from highly advanced civilizations cooperates to restrict ET races with a hostile agenda when they break Universal Law. All of us are entitled to free will, including participating in life as perpetrators and victims. However, many believe that the corruption on this planet has gone much too far. Earth needs help. So, when "service to self" beings cross the line, legions of "service to others" beings bring assistance.

- Supporting these theories, and in alignment with the reduction of reported abductions, several channellings say that any negative ETs that do exist out there have been evicted and excommunicated from Earth since sometime in the 1990s.

- Let's forget theories and look at this from a law of attraction standpoint. People who are drawn to making contact are already vibrating at a high level and contact with beings of a lower vibration is simply not a match. Think about it: anyone willing to look like a wingnut and try CE-5 demonstrates a first-class level of fearlessness.

- Lastly, in a group of people, the level of contact is generally limited to the "lowest common denominator." For example, if one person is ready to make direct face-to-face contact, but the rest of the group is not, then it doesn't happen. Think about this in reverse. If one person is of a much lower vibration than a bunch of happy people, the power of the happier people equalizes things and excludes the possibility of interacting with a badass ET or a negative entity.

Ultimately, you must make a decision about what your reality will be. Life is a tremendous buffet of contrasts for good reason: for you to be able to choose. Accept that negativity of all kinds is a part of life that we learn from so we can create the reality we want. This is your show! Take care of yourself and your own growth, do a clearing if you feel unwell, and hang out with positive, happy, kind people. Above all, trust your senses. Feel out the vibe of every situation that comes your way. You'll know whether to turn from it or towards it. You got this.

"I'm still fearful"

Don't force it. See *Not Up To Speed*, the first segment of this section.

> Tip: If you give credence to channellings, use your discernment to ensure you are getting good information… some channellings are vulnerable to bad interference or are simply not clearly received.

A SIGHTING IN SIX OUTINGS

We believe that if you focus on the three key ingredients:

1. Connection to One Mind Consciousness
2. A Sincere Heart
3. Clear Intention

You'll have a sighting within six outings.

If you can get out with a few other people, all the better. Try some of the suggestions in the book. You don't need any laser pointers or radar scanners—just you out under the stars.

When you get your sightings, do share! What you saw, internal experiences, what your process was... Jump on ETLet'sTalk or a Facebook group page and dish it!

- ETLet'sTalk: http://etletstalk.com/
- The CE-5 Initiative: https://www.facebook.com/groups/205824492783376/
- CE-5, UFO, SIRIUS: ETLetsTalk.com: https://www.facebook.com/groups/1593375944256413/
- CE-5 Universal Global Mission: https://www.facebook.com/groups/1827858540868714/
- CE-5 Initiative Working Groups Global: https://www.facebook.com/groups/1591401614435784/?fref=gs&dti=205824492783376&hc_location=group

If you followed the instructions in this handbook, and you did not get a sighting in six outings, give us an email. Let's figure out what your resistance is.

calgaryce5@gmail.com

As James Gilliland says,
"Contact starts from within."
We hope this handbook
inspires you to take action and
expand your inner self.

Yearly UFO Sightings: 1910 - 2010

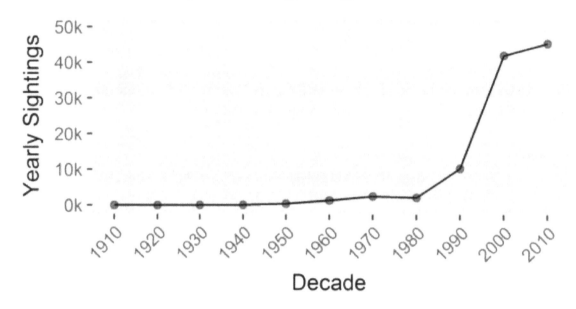

Data from: National UFO Reporting Centre
Compiled by: Sam Montford

PART THREE:

OPINION EDITORIAL/

APPENDIX-LIKE STUFF

FALSE FLAGS

If you're skeptical and have made it this far, we commend you for your ability to tolerate different perspectives. Whatever ultimate reality is, you demonstrate a level of evolution that we believe will contribute to sightings! Now… let's test you further.

A 'false flag' is a terrorist act that is perpetrated upon one's own citizens to unite them against an outside enemy and distract them from the real threat, which actually comes from within the homeland.

Werner Von Braun was a German aerospace engineer who was brought to the United States after WWII as part of Operation Paperclip. His assistant describes his warnings to her about a false flag of epic proportions:

> "What was most interesting to me was a repetitive sentence that he said to me over and over again during the approximately four years that I had the opportunity to work with him. He said the strategy that was being used to educate the public and decision makers was to use scare tactics… first the Russians are going to be considered to be the enemy. In fact, in 1974, they were the enemy, the identified enemy…Then terrorists would be identified, and that was soon to follow. We heard a lot about terrorism. Then we were going to identify third-world country 'crazies.' We now call them Nations of Concern…The next enemy was asteroids. Now, at this point he kind of chuckled the first time he said it. 'Asteroids—against asteroids we are going to build space-based weapons.' And the funniest one of all was what he called aliens, extraterrestrials. That would be the final scare. And over and over and over during the four years that I knew him and was giving speeches for him, he would bring up that last card. 'And remember Carol, the last card is the alien card. We are going to have to build space-based weapons against aliens and all of it is a lie.'"
>
> —Carol Rosin

Dr. Greer has also received insider information about the possibility of the Military Industrial Complex hoaxing an "Alien Invasion" to fortify power and justify their existence.

Supporting a parallel, similar, possibility, Barbara Marciniak has channelled about a predicted time when an ET race takes over as our new leaders and that we, in our foolishness, revere them like Gods.

Luckily for us, the mere existence of the *Unacknowledged* documentary now makes a serious dent in either of these nefarious possibilities. If a farce like either of these start rolling, it won't take much work for people to share the documentary with loved ones to empower the community with knowledge. That, and CE-5 groups around the world can contact local media and provide evidence of their experience communicating with benevolent beings. You may want to record your process, collect footage and keep reports of healings just for this purpose.

Since 2001, Carol Rosin has been engaged in political activism to stop the weaponization of space. Carol has spearheaded *The Treaty on Prevention of the Placement of Weapons in Outer Space.* Your best contribution is a letter in your own words, which is forwarded to Presidents of Nation States around the world. For more information go to http://peaceinspace.com.

FRIDAY

A fellow Albertan and CE-5 leader, Charles Brygdes, says that every week he thinks, "Maybe this is the Friday when disclosure happens!" He focuses on this day because Richard Dolan, UFO researcher, has proposed that disclosure will happen on a day when the stock market can be closed for a few days as the world reels in shock (and hopefully stabilizes a bit). Disclosure may have effects that are uncomfortable or challenging. For this reason, governments the world over are leaking documents out slowly to help us get used to the new paradigm.

"When will disclosure happen?"
That's a good question. Richard Dolan has said that there is a 90% chance that it will happen within twenty years and that his prediction is conservative. (His quote is from 2016, so that calculates out to 2036.) Bashar, as channelled via Daryl Anka, predicts that it will be between the years 2030 and 2033. Bashar does not make predictions often or lightly, and did predict 9/11 right up to the year. This guesswork, of course, is relative to our own personal actions. How will you contribute to disclosure?

"What about 'them' – what if 'they' won't let disclosure happen?"
We know that the criminals currently wielding power at the helm of the world are trying to supress disclosure to uphold this oppressive slave labour tyranny. How do we know they won't succeed with their false flags and obfuscation?

Let Bill Brockbrader's story tell the answer. Bill was an above-top secret military specialist who flew Tomahawk missiles into small Afghanistan villages during non-war time. Bill came to realize that what he was doing was wrong and he eventually extricated himself from service. He then became a member of Anonymous. Edward Snowden, famous-former-CIA-computer-guy who gave us the truth about the NSA, was also part of the same Anonymous cell. Edward needed a decoy, because when something happens in the outside world that excites intelligence agencies, internal security goes down. In the Anonymous cell, everyone said: Obviously, the decoy has to be Bill – he has the best story. So Bill stepped up. When Bill did his interview with Kerry Cassidy exposing these war crimes, Edward snuck out terabytes of data and booked it to an asylum. (Thank You Russia!) Bill was seized, sentenced to a term in jail, and then when he was released, he went underground. His story is truly heroic. Now that you have the context of who Bill is, here is the juicy part (like all that wasn't juicy enough?): Back when Bill was working for the military, they asked him to do a side project because of his high intelligence and psychic ability. He was asked to look at Project Looking Glass, which was a device that the MIC previously used to predict the future. They asked him, "Which timeline will win?" Bill poured over the data and gave them the answer: All potential timelines have collapsed into one timeline; only one outcome now exists. The rest of what happens here on earth is like the endgame in chess where the loser, instead of resigning to a confirmed loss with dignity, is scrambling to extend their reign. Spoiler alert: The good guys win.

I can personally vouch for Bill's tireless partner, Eva Moore, a fellow Canadian, who is a whistleblower and activist in her own right. I have known her for many years and she is one of the most earnest, bravest, strongest women I know.

Whether it is this Friday or 982 Fridays from now, disclosure is going to happen!

FREE ENERGY

There's a really good YouTube video interview with Daryl Anka about Ascension and the New World Order (https://www.youtube.com/watch?v=vRtbvXp3wkw). Here is a summary with some of our additional thoughts:

- No one has you under control.

- Once you realize your own power and raise your frequency, your most desired manifestations will unfold. (Or, if you look at it another way, you will change frequencies and move to an improved parallel universe.)

- Basically, anything we fight against we anchor to our reality.

- The more we focus on what we don't want, the more we experience them.

- For things to change, we must PREFER a reality rather than NEED it.

- When we want something desperately it keeps moving away from us and we keep chasing after it.

- There is no one "keeping" free energy from us. We don't need disclosure to get to free energy. Many people have created free energy devices. Some people have their devices confiscated, labs burned down, or are killed. Some have created free energy and have not had their methods arrested. (Someone in our group has seen a free energy demonstration in Quebec by Daniel Pomerleau. No one has been able to understand or replicate it to date! We think that he may be using his own energy field or consciousness technology as a catalyst, which may be why his device has not been taken.) Confiscated or not, our scientists will receive the inspiration to create them again, as well as the correct intuition guiding us to how to do it safely. When we are in tune with Source, the right ideas will arrive at the right times.

- Fear draws what you don't want towards you like a magnet, but a little caution is a good thing. Here is what we have heard about safely developing free energy. Once you turn a free energy device on, scanning technology can locate where that energy is being created. And, thanks to Edward Snowden, we know "they" can track every digital action you take. Reputedly, it doesn't even matter if your phone is turned off. We've also heard that there are satellite cameras that can zoom live into your neighbourhood. That is a bit of a puzzle to get around, but it can and will be creatively solved.

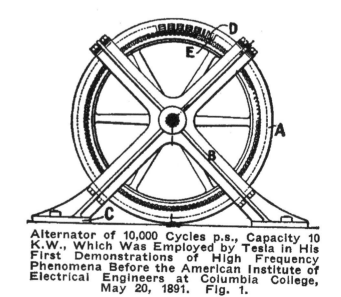

Alternator of 10,000 Cycles p.s., Capacity 10 K.W., Which Was Employed by Tesla in His First Demonstrations of High Frequency Phenomena Before the American Institute of Electrical Engineers at Columbia College, May 20, 1891. Fig. 1.

CHANGING THE WORLD

You don't actually need to save the world. We don't NEED disclosure. We are here to grow. The earth could shatter into a million pieces and, tragic as that would be, it would ultimately be ok. Maybe there's a parallel world where this has already happened. Maybe there are earths where the Golden Age is already in full force. (How did we get stuck here?) That kind of takes the pressure off doesn't it? We are eternal and exploring and being in every reality, every outcome.

What about uplifting humanity? Giving of yourself is a by-product of your expansion. It feels good. So as we expand we are compelled to give more. It is a natural impulse and the outcome of your evolution. As you expand, you will understand that we are all one and an injustice done to one is an injustice done to all. You will realize you really are everyone and everything. It's a funny paradox because although you will compulsively begin acting more on behalf of the all, you will also realize you do not need to worry about the other "you's" on their own journey, or the outcome of all this. Each person still has their own free will. You can't control anyone. Focus on yourself, enjoy it all, and it will all turn out perfectly in the end, even if it doesn't.

Whatever you do, don't rail against what you don't want. Judgment anchors what you hate to your reality. The key to getting to where you want to be is to **Prefer** instead of **Need**. So when you think about the Federal Reserve, and the criminal tyranny and enslavement they have so masterfully manipulated, just say to yourself, "I prefer...(insert your preference here)." However, if you feel angst towards that syndicate, you give away your power. And maybe you will also skip around to some parallel reality where Iceland did not already kick their asses out of their country (Yes, they did it, and we can too!). As the adage goes: What you fear the most draws towards you like a magnet. Yuck.

What to do? Take inspired action—do what excites you! Realize we are all one, and when you want power, freedom, or sovereignty for yourself, act on behalf of all in the spirit of love and we will all get there together and claim all that has been ours all along. Carve out the role you want in this exciting time and above all, enjoy the process. Life is meant to be FUN!

We want to share with you our preference: that you do whatever you feel called to do, and you walk that path despite fear, ignoring the opinions of all others, including whatever we are selling you on our own soap box. However, you did pick up this document. So, we think you might want to be a part of the vision we can clearly see for our future. We would love it if you made CE-5 a part of your life, because #1, we know first hand how fun it is, and #2, it would be great if more people would spread the knowledge that ETs are real to all our loved ones, with first hand eye witness testimony as proof.

We don't need disclosure to happen faster, but it sure would be nice, wouldn't it? Let's be part of a reality where disclosure happens sooner than later, and all of us can experience the abundance we deserve.

THE PEOPLE'S DISCLOSURE MOVEMENT

How can we help disclosure unfold? The People's Disclosure Movement is an initiative organized by a group of people who have realized the power of the contribution of the common man and have given voice to it in form. Kosta Makreas founded this movement in Oct 2010. The movement has activated thousands of people all over the world. It has transformed people from "Believers" into "Knowers." It has resulted in people taking back their power from the authorities. Part of that movement is "The Global CE-5 Initiative" a.k.a. "ETLet'sTalk" which has been putting ET Contact teams in the field monthly since its inception in 2010. You can flock with this fine-feathered community by registering at http://etletstalk.com/.

You are an influential and integral part of disclosure. The UFO topic can be a hot one. You will really agitate yourself going around "convincing" people of your truth. Don't bother – it's a waste of time. From a universal law based perspective that would be anchoring those people and this reality to you anyways—whatever it is you fight against, you handcuff to yourself.

What you can do is become an ambassador of humanity. And it's easy:

- Hold a CE-5 meeting every month.

- When your family, friends and co-workers ask you what you did on the weekend, tell them. When you do CE-5 regularly, you always have some kind of UFO news to share.

- Share who you are and what your passions are freely. I often tell people when I first meet them that I am a UFO nut.

That's all! How does this work? First of all it puts the words UFO, ET, CE-5 etc., in the daily vernacular of our consciousness as a whole. Every casual mention legitimizes the movement.

Secondly, your story is important. For the average person, when you drop your story and you're not proselytizing, it's enticing and interesting. Most people believe we are not alone in the universe. In smaller numbers (but somehow louder) are the skeptics, who are not going to be convinced even in the face of the irrefutable documents that governments are releasing. However, when you say you saw an unexplainable light in the sky moving in a way that no other conventional human made craft could move, with other witnesses, and you were not high, a fault line occurs in their reality. It's a slowly moving crack, but these planted seeds are important.

How Kosta was inspired to start The People's Disclosure and the ensuing network ETLet'sTalk:

"In July of 2010, after almost 4 years of immersion in CE-5 training with a LOT of successful ET Contact, I knew there were hundreds, maybe thousands of people just like me around the world who were doing the same.

"I had an inspiration: why not connect all of us into a coherent community? Maybe that would synergize our efforts. I asked my spiritual guidance if it was worth the time, energy and effort to 'organize' so many on such a scale.

"I was startled to receive telepathic communication from what I recognized by that time as an ET source:

'Create as many contact teams as possible, in as many places as possible, as soon as possible.'

...came the words into my mind.

'"What will that accomplish?' I asked.

'As more humans ask to see us in the skies, this will give us permission and opportunity to appear in many more places all around your world. This will result in even more humans seeing us...who will then ask on a greater scale to see us. This will allow us to appear in even more places, and so on. We call this a 'virtuous circle'. Someday the evidence of our presence in your world's skies will be too overwhelming to deny.'

"I was startled at this information, yet very, very happy. Their request was simple, clear and direct!"

Dr. Greer encourages the same. Disclosure is no longer in control of the governments or the cartels. It's already happening and it is up to us to free ourselves. Greer inspires each of us to action with a saying that was drilled into students at medical school:

"Learn one, do one, teach one"

We join our voices to this chorus in invitation to you: start a team and teach others how to start their own teams. Be part of one of the biggest, most exciting movements that will help bring peace to this planet.

BEWARE OF DIVISION

We are all one. When we condemn someone, we hurt ourselves.

When you hear someone criticize another, remember that all attack is a call for help. Forgive the attacker. Say something uplifting about the person who was criticized. Refocus attention to healing the attacker. What do they need? Most people just want love. Love them.

As you grow into your own enlightenment you will love everyone. Even Hitler. This is because as we evolve, we become more inclusive and less exclusive. We also understand ultimate reality better: that we come into this form and do horrible things to each other, knowing that in the end the outcome is assured and it was all just a play for us to experience who we really are. We are Love. Who is to say that your worst enemy is not your most precious lover playing their part in this lifetime perfectly?

Do you think someone is stupid, evil, or even a dis-info agent? Bless them, then ignore them. Let them lead their nutty life. Do you think you have never had a past life where you were just as un-evolved? Guaranteed we have all done heinous things in past lives long ago. Horrible things that if we had an awareness of them we would not sleep for the rest of our days.

Anytime anyone condemns anyone else, contact moves farther away. This applies to everyone. Who did you wrong? Your mother, brother, or ex-lover? Wow—have we all ever got work to do!

"To get open contact we need to get much more cohesive and stop fighting... refusing to raise our vibration is a decision to not make contact with a civilization that is vibrating much higher than us."
- Daryl Anka/Bashar

"If we do not unite in our similarities, we will dissolve in our differences"
- Samoiya Shelley Yates

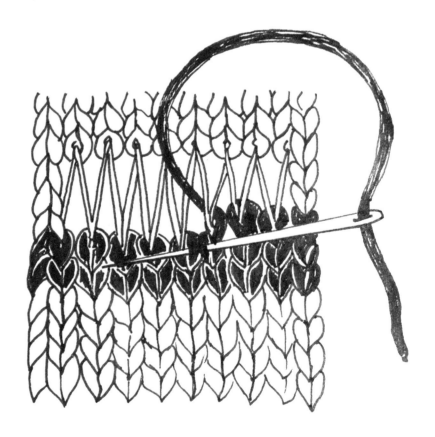

HOW TO DESTROY A MOVEMENT

If the general populace become aware that free energy exists, energy, financial and power systems will crumble. Those currently in power use many avenues to maintain their prosperity and control. Agencies such as the Joint Threat Research Intelligence Group (JTRIG) run programs to ruin reputations that tarnish the truth and destroy movements. They have mottos like: "The 4 D's: Deny, Disrupt, Degrade, and Deceive."

Some of their techniques:

- "Among the core self-identified purposes of JTRIG are two tactics: (1) to inject all sorts of false material onto the internet in order to destroy the reputation of its targets; and (2) to use social sciences and other techniques to manipulate online discourse and activism to generate outcomes it considers desirable."

- 'Honey traps' (luring people into compromising situations using sex).

- 'False flag operations' (posting material to the internet and falsely attributing it to someone else).

- Fake victim blog posts (pretending to be a victim of the individual whose reputation they want to destroy), and posting "negative information" on various forums.

Take a look at this slide, part of instructional material to teach agents to "game" outcomes. We believe the CE-5 world has already been targeted. To keep this movement strong, we must focus on our shared ideology, common beliefs, and band together against those that do not want freedom for all.

SECRET//SI//REL TO USA, FVEY

Identifying & Exploiting fracture points

Things that push a group together

Shared opposition

Shared ideology

Common beliefs

Tension

Personal power

Pre-existing cleavages

Competition

Ideological differences

Things that pull a group apart

https://theintercept.com/2014/02/24/jtrig-manipulation/

THE FUTURE

I'm going to leave you with a short story about my 7-year-old son being introduced to ET. We were in Banff National Park, bundled up to go stargazing together for the first time. We were looking at the Milky Way and he was loving the laser pointer. He said it was like a light sabre going forever into space. I saw a falling star (or streaker) and pointed out to him where it had been. He had never seen a falling star before and I was hoping he might see another one that night, but I thought, *How is he going to see one when they go by so quickly?* At his age it takes a lot of time to filter in information from the world and a tiny quick light like that would be very difficult to catch. As we were looking up at the constellations, I told him that we are also looking for UFOs, and that they look like camera flashes. He got very excited and said "Hello Aliens!" to the sky and then not a moment later I saw a flashbulb! With the laser pointer, I circled the location where the flashbulb had appeared and when he focused on that spot we both saw about 5 or 6 more, in quick succession. We were so excited, squealing and laughing and shouting in the dark. He asked if this is what I did and I said, "Yes." He said he didn't know it was so much fun. We said, "Thank You" and continued pointing out constellations. When he got cold, we got ready to go and I said, "Bye everyone!" to the sky. He looked up, waved and said "Bye!" Immediately one more big flashbulb! What with his yet developing ability to catch a quick flash like that he missed it, but as soon as I pointed out to him where it had been, a falling star went by. His first falling star. (Or streaker!) I got my wish for him. He made a wish for himself, and we went inside.

Imagine the world we are helping to create for our children, who are already ready to receive it.

With love for you all,
Cielia and the Calgary CE-5 Group

CE-5 LOG TEMPLATES

Use the templates on the following pages to keep track of your fieldwork. If you have fulfilled the three key elements (1. Connection to One Mind Consciousness, 2. A Sincere Heart, 3. Clear Intention) we believe you will have had at least one sighting by the time you have filled all six logs out.

CE-5 Log 1
Date: _____
Location: _____
Start/End Time: _____

In Attendance:
_____
_____

Agenda:
_____ _____
_____ _____
_____ _____
_____ _____
_____ _____
_____ _____
_____ _____
_____ _____

Int./Ext. Experiences or Sightings:
_____
_____
_____
_____
_____
_____
_____
_____
_____
_____
_____
_____
_____
_____
_____
_____
_____
_____
_____
_____
_____
_____
_____
_____
_____

CE-5 Log 2

Date: _____

Location: _____

Start/End Time: _____

In Attendance:

_____

_____

Agenda:

_____	_____
_____	_____
_____	_____
_____	_____
_____	_____
_____	_____
_____	_____

Int./Ext. Experiences or Sightings:

_____

_____

_____

_____

_____

_____

_____

_____

_____

_____

_____

_____

_____

_____

_____

_____

_____

_____

_____

_____

_____

CE-5 Log 3
Date: _____
Location: _____
Start/End Time: _____

In Attendance:

_____
_____

Agenda:

_____	_____
_____	_____
_____	_____
_____	_____
_____	_____
_____	_____
_____	_____

Int./Ext. Experiences or Sightings:

_____
_____
_____
_____
_____
_____
_____
_____
_____
_____
_____
_____
_____
_____
_____
_____
_____
_____
_____
_____
_____
_____
_____
_____

CE-5 Log 4

Date: _____

Location: _____

Start/End Time: _____

In Attendance:

_____

_____

Agenda:

_____   _____

_____   _____

_____   _____

_____   _____

_____   _____

_____   _____

_____   _____

Int./Ext. Experiences or Sightings:

_____

_____

_____

_____

_____

_____

_____

_____

_____

_____

_____

_____

_____

_____

_____

_____

_____

_____

_____

_____

_____

_____

_____

_____

_____

CE-5 Log 5
Date: _____
Location: _____
Start/End Time: _____

In Attendance:
_____
_____

Agenda:
_____ _____
_____ _____
_____ _____
_____ _____
_____ _____
_____ _____
_____ _____

Int./Ext. Experiences or Sightings:
_____
_____
_____
_____
_____
_____
_____
_____
_____
_____
_____
_____
_____
_____
_____
_____
_____
_____
_____
_____
_____
_____
_____
_____
_____

CE-5 Log 6
Date: _____
Location: _____
Start/End Time: _____

In Attendance:
_____
_____

Agenda:

_____   _____
_____   _____
_____   _____
_____   _____
_____   _____
_____   _____
_____   _____

Int./Ext. Experiences or Sightings:

_____
_____
_____
_____
_____
_____
_____
_____
_____
_____
_____
_____
_____
_____
_____
_____
_____
_____
_____
_____
_____
_____
_____

WHO'S WHO IN THE ZOO

There are a number of major contributors in the world of contact and/or CE-5. Many of these people are running current efforts to communicate with ET and you can join them on a retreat.

Sixto Paz Wells - Spain and Latin America
Sixto started Rahma in 1974, the first modern, structured, international ET contact group. Rahma was formed with the mission of bridging ET civilizations with human beings in the best interest for the planet and humanity. Sixto is known for summoning the international press to ten sightings in advance of their occurrence. The Spanish world of ufology is different than the English world: information about ETs presence on earth is much more available on the Spanish web and contact has been closer and more direct. This is likely a result of the structure of their direct, clear and consistent language, which reflects the culture's consciousness as a whole, and their readiness for contact. http://www.sixtopazwells.com/

Enrique Villanueva - West Coast, USA
Enrique joined Rahma in 1988 and started a satellite group in Los Angeles in 2009. Currently, Enrique works as a professional hypnotherapist in California and runs a contact retreat at Mt. Shasta every summer, based on the Rahma contact protocols. We don't know much about Enrique, so let this quote speak for him. He says, "They (ET) say that the most important contact is not the contact with them, but the contact within. Once you reach that level then the contact with them is a consequence of your preparation. So they are always open and waiting for us to reach that level and then they will trigger the experience for you. It's an invitation to expand our consciousness. And they are already here. We don't need ambassadors. Every single human being can be an ambassador."
https://www.facebook.com/enrique.villanueva.56,
http://enriquevillanueva.weebly.com/

Dr. Steven M. Greer - Southeastern USA
Steven Greer, MD was an emergency room doctor whose life took an unexpected turn into the world of ET, government corruption, cover up, black ops, man-made spacecraft, confiscated free energy devices, whistleblowers and informants. He taught the CE-5 protocol through the group CSETI beginning in 1990. He is brilliant, energetic and intensely loyal to his often-challenging path. He spearheaded The Disclosure Project in 2001, has published several books and he has also produced two major documentaries. http://siriusdisclosure.com/

Lyssa Royal Holt - Arizona, Japan
Lyssa was an original member of CSETI circa the 90s and moved on to lead a contact team in Arizona where she and her group received more information about contact methodology through her channelling process. Since 2010 her group has been working with entering and working within quantum states of consciousness. Her book, *Prepare for Contact*, is an essential manual describing the intimate connection between sightings and the development of your consciousness. You can attend trainings and special events with her in Arizona, Japan, and other locations.
 http://www.lyssaroyal.net/

James Gilliland - Pacific Northwest USA

James is the founder of ECETI (Enlightened Contact with ET Intelligence), which is located on land in the wilds of Washington State where a long history of UFO sightings go back hundreds of years. It is otherwise known as "The Ranch," and has been around for several decades. Mount Adams is nearby and may have an intergalactic ET base inside—we know someone who saw a door open in the mountain and then saw UFOs flying in and out! James is kind, personable and full of dad jokes. To visit The Ranch one must first request a private invitation—go to his website. http://www.eceti.org/

Kosta Makreas - West Coast, USA

Kosta is the glue of the CE-5 world. He has been making successful ET Contact since 2006, and along the way has hatched The People's Disclosure Movement, The Global CE-5 Initiative and the ETLet'sTalk Community. The ETLet'sTalk Community has over 20,000 members in 100+ countries. (For more on this important network see the section describing The People's Disclosure) He has dedicated his life to spreading awareness and hope through his projects by facilitating empowerment through community for the common man. He is noble and down-to-earth all at the same time. His lovely partner Hollis Polk co-creates with him as she expertly teaches people how to recognize and develop their natural psychic powers in order to create a better ET Contact experience. They are a power couple to be reckoned with. http://etletstalk.com/

Smaller Fries But We Love These Guys

Mark Koprowski – Tokyo, Japan

Originally from Minnesota, Mark has been running CE-5 events in Japan since 2013. He has been on a number of contact retreats all over the world and knows who is doing what and where. Mark has given our group lots of great advice, much of which is in this handbook and which has helped us greatly with our progress. Mark has also helped as a contributor for this book. If you visit his group's website or Facebook page, you'll find some interesting articles, videos and CE-5 field reports relevant to anyone practising CE-5 anywhere in the world. http://www.ce5tokyo.org

Deb Warren - OCSETI (Okanagan Centre for Study of ET Intelligence), Western Canada

Deb is our mentor from the province next door, and runs her CE-5 group out of Vernon, BC. We met her on one of her numerous CE-5 tours of Western Canada, where she generously spent her summers going from group to group over many kilometres to share her knowledge and do fieldwork with newbies. She has been on more Dr. Greer retreats than you can count on two hands, and she has always made herself freely available for help and support. We're very grateful for all the phone calls and emails she has responded to. She helped us greatly with this handbook and filled a notable gap in the equipment section. https://ocseti.wordpress.com/

RECOMMENDED MEDIA

Books

- *Preparing for Contact* (Lyssa Royal Holt)
- *Calling on Extraterrestrials* (Lisette Larkins)
- *Paths to Contact* (Jeff Becker)
- *The E.T. Contact Experience – CE-5 Handbook* (Peter Maxwell Slattery)
- *Evolution Through Contact* (Don Daniels)
- *Forbidden Truth, Hidden Knowledge* (Steven M. Greer)
- *Contact: Countdown to Transformation* (Steven M. Greer)
- *Unacknowledged* (Steven M. Greer & Steve Alten)
- *Exopolitics: Political Implications Of The Extraterrestrial Presence* (Michael E. Salla)
- *Galactic Diplomacy: Getting to Yes with ET* (Michael E. Salla)
- *Bringers of the Dawn* (Barbara Marciniak)
- *Becoming Gods* (James Gilliland)
- *The Orb Project* (Miceal Ledwith & Klaus Heinemann)
- *From Venus I Came* (Omnec Onec)
- *The Hathor Material* (Tom Kenyon)
- *Secrets of the Lost Mode of Prayer* (Gregg Braden)
- *Walking Between the Worlds* (Gregg Braden)
- *Electrogravitics Systems* (Thomas Valone, PhD.)
- *Defying Gravity* (T. Townsend Brown)
- *Love* (Leo Buscalia)
- *Conversations with God, Book 4 – Awaken the Species* (Neale Donald Walsch)

Podcasts

- *CE-5 Minneapolis* hosted by Paul Riedner. 13 episodes produced.
- *As You Wish Talk Radio* hosted by James Gilliland.
- *Becoming a Cosmic Citizen* hosted by Sierra Neblina & Don Daniels.
- *Fade to Black* hosted by Jimmy Church.
- *Opens Mind UFO Radio*
- *The Grimerica Show* hosted by Graham & Darren.
  Graham has been with our CE-5 group for years. He and Darren are on the frontier of exploration, diving into a wide range of fascinating topics such as: consciousness, UFOs, ancient mysteries, alternative realities, etc. The pre-amble to each interview is worth it alone for the banter and jingles. Guests include: Stanton Friedman, Jacques Vallee, Richard Dolan, Joseph Farrell and many more. Be sure to listen to episode #243 with Grant Cameron and #220 with Kosta and Hollis.

Websites & YouTube

- **ET Let's Talk** - Mentioned many times in this document, ET Let's Talk has a treasure trove of CE-5 reports, CE-5 groups, and more. ETLet'sTalk also showcases Danny Sheehan's webinars. Danny is a constitutional and public interest lawyer, public speaker, political activist and educator. He talks about Cosmic Humanity, meditation and consciousness, and related topics on a regular schedule. http://etletstalk.com/
- **Sirius Disclosure** - Dr. Greer's central hub. http://www.siriusdisclosure.com/

- **Center for the Study of Extraterrestrial Intelligence (CSETI)** http://www.cseti.org/
- **Enlightened Contact with Extraterrestrial Intelligence (ECETI)** http://www.eceti.org/
- **ECETI Australia** - The CE-5 resource down under headed by Peter Maxwell Slattery. https://www.ecetiaustralia.org/
- **Peter Maxwell Slattery** - Another website for Peter. https://www.petermaxwellslattery.com/
- **The Pete N Rae Pathways Show** topics include: CE5, Consciousness, nonhuman intelligences, and the multi-spectrum of phenomena related to contact. https://www.youtube.com/channel/UCEdJ75f6ipFbKdUjGeGzMQQ
- **CE-5 Aotearoa** - Non-profit organization based in New Zealand. New Zealand and International events for CE-5 and related modalities. https://www.ce5.nz/
- **JCETI Japan** - Japan Center for Extraterrestrial Intelligence headed by Greg Sullivan. Japanese: http://www.jceti.org/, English: http://www.ce5-japan.com
- **Daryl Anka** - Channeller of an ET entity named Bashar. http://www.bashar.org/
- **Tom Kenyon** - Channeller of a group of ET called the Hathors. http://tomkenyon.com/
- **Dr. Edgar Mitchell** - An astronaut who started FREE (Foundation for Research into Extraterrestrial Encounters). http://www.experiencer.org/
- **Richard Dolan** - Considered by many to be the foremost author and speaker on the UFO topic today. https://www.richarddolanpress.com/
- **Samoiya Shelley Yates** – This Canadian East Coaster had a near death experience where she met ETs who told her how to miraculously save her son's life and help anchor the planet at a critical time by facilitating group meditations bringing together millions of people. https://www.youtube.com/watch?v=KHGyu_AXNWg&t=6
- **Grant Cameron** - Hyper-speed Canadian UFO researcher. Interesting, intelligent and entertaining. http://www.presidentialufo.com/
- **Michael Schratt** - Black Ops, ARVs and UFOs. https://www.youtube.com/watch?time_continue=3&v=b-uufP375zE (9 mins) https://www.youtube.com/watch?v=pFWza6LTMrY (1.5 hours)

Documentaries & Other Media

- *Unacknowledged* (2017) The first documentary to watch. UFO cover up 101 (On Netflix).
- *Sirius* (2012) Although produced earlier, watch this one second. Includes CE-5s and genetic study of a mummified ET body. https://www.youtube.com/watch?v=5C_-HLD21hA
- *Contact Has Begun: A True Story with James Gilliland* (2008) https://www.youtube.com/watch?v=V261_HKD4aQ
- *CSETI Working Group Training Materials* http://new.cseti.org/members-section/51-art-cseti-working-group-training-materials.html
- **TODO ES ENERGIA** (Everything Is Energy) Gustavo, a member of our Calgary CE-5 group, has a Spanish speaking Facebook group uncovering all kinds of information about the connection of body, mind and soul, including: awakening, conspiracies, yoga, extraterrestrials, Reiki, prana healing, crystals, tarot, meditations, remote viewing, astral projection, lucid dreams, energy, physical and quantum mechanical and acupuncture. Search Facebook with the group name to find and join. https://www.facebook.com/groups/838503992965283/

GLOSSARY OF TERMS

A

Alien Reproduction Vehicles (ARV): Ships made by humans, reverse engineered from crashed UFOs

aliens: Beings not from "here"

alleged meteor a.k.a. 'streaker': A shooting star that might be a UFO

alleged satellite: A satellite that might be a UFO

alleged star: A star with anomalous characteristics that might be a UFO

ambassador: A representative for a group

ancient mystery schools: Organizations that hold and protect sacred teachings

angelic beings: Beings that are heavenly/spiritual/like an angel

anomalous light: A light that behaves in a way that cannot be conventionally explained

Arcturians: Small, greenish blue advanced beings with three fingers, and almond shaped eyes

ARVs: Ships made by humans, reverse engineered from crashed UFOs

ascended masters: Beings who have attained enlightenment

ascension: Spiritual evolution

astral body: A part of you that is energy that can travel independently from your physical body

atmospheric refraction: Twinkling of stars near the horizon due to layers of turbulent air

aurora: Delightful natural light display occurring close to the poles

Avian Beings: Tall, blue feathered, avian and humanoid advanced beings

B

Becker-Hagens grid: A grid that overlays the earth, where special energy points converge

bio-break: A break in the evening's proceedings to attend to human biological needs

black-ops: Military projects that are absorbing obscene amounts of tax dollars

brahmin consciousness: A state of mind equal to the divine incarnate

C

CE-1: Close encounter of the first kind (Seeing an ET craft within 500 feet)

CE-2: Close encounter of the second kind (Physical evidence of a landing or craft)

CE-3: Close encounter of the third kind (Seeing a being)

CE-4: Close encounter of the fourth kind (Interaction with beings/surreal encounters/abduction)

CE-5: Close encounter of the fifth kind (Human-initiated communication with ET)

celestial beings: Beings from other realities such as spirits, angels, ascended masters

celestial: From the sky

chakras: Energy centres in the body going up the spine and up through the head

channelling: Where someone relays communication from another being (ET or non-physical)

clairaudience: Hearing something beyond normal sensory ability

clairgustance: Tasting something beyond normal sensory ability

clairscent: Smelling something beyond normal sensory ability

clairsentience: Feeing non-physical sensations or energy in the body

clairvoyance: Perceiving something beyond normal sensory ability

cloud busting: Trying to shape or move clouds with intention

consciousness: Love. Or awareness. Or expansion. Or God. Or …

cosmic consciousness: The collective consciousness of the universe itself

cosmos: The universe, especially a harmonious, well ordered one

crop circle tones: Anomalous sounds recorded in a crop circle

crop circle: Geometric patterns in farmer's fields with anomalous, reshaped plant nodes

crown chakra: Energy centre situated at the top of the head

CSETI: Center for the Study of Extraterrestrial Intelligence, founded by Dr. Steven Greer

D

didgeridoo: An Australian musical wind instrument made from a hollow branch

dimensions: Different realities/worlds, can be categorized as 3D, 4D, 5D etc

dis-info agent: A liar who accepts money to spread untruths to deceive people

disclosure: When the truth about ET is revealed

Disclosure Project, The: A CSETI campaign that disclosed info about ET to the public

distorted sky: Anomalous appearance of a portion of the sky (Heat waves, shimmering, darker)

download: Energy or information brought into your awareness, knowledge or physical body

drone: An aerial vehicle controlled remotely by a human on the ground

E

ECETI: Enlightened Contact with Extraterrestrial Intelligence – James Gilliland's group of seekers

emissary: Someone sent on a special mission, usually as a diplomatic representative

energy download: Energy meant to heal, empower or upgrade

energy: Unseen moving or pulsing power, what we are made of, how life works

ET: Extraterrestrial

ETLet'sTalk: Networking site for people excited about CE-5

expansion: Description of coming to awareness about one's true nature

external communication: Received information from other beings that occur in 3D reality

extraterrestrial: A being that does not originate from earth

F

fast walker: NORAD term for a fast satellite, a missile or a speedy UFO

Federal Reserve: A private corporation that has devised a sanctioned way to steal your money

fieldwork: CE-5 work done outside in nature

flashbulb: A small flash in the sky like a camera flash, like a star swiftly appearing and disappearing

free energy: The ability to capture the endless energy around us

FREE: Dr. Edgar Mitchell's Foundation for Research into Extraterrestrial Encounters

frequency: The rate at which our elemental parts move, where high vibes = love, low vibes = fear

G

gaia: A personified name describing our living planet

geo-stationary orbit: In sync with the earth (To observers below the object has no movement)

Global CE-5 Initiative, The: A movement facilitating monthly unified global CE-5s

golden age: Future era on earth with utopic characteristics

Great Spirit: An indigenous term for a universal spiritual force (Creator, God, etc.)

H

Hathors: Advanced beings, humanoid, masters of sound, with delicate fan like ears
heart chakra: Energy centre at the heart
Hubble telescope: One of the largest and most versatile telescopes launched into space
military spacecraft: Ships made by humans reverse engineered from crashed UFOs
hybrid: A being that is part human and part other being
hyper-jump: Travelling faster than light
hypnogogic state: The transitional state of being while falling asleep or waking up

I

inter-dimensional: Having the ability to move between worlds/realities/dimensions
internal communication: Received information from other beings that occur internally
International Space Station (ISS): A research station orbiting space that contains people
Interplanetary Council: An assembly of ET ambassadors providing governance and legislation
interstellar: "Between stars", often used to denote vast space, and travelling through it
Iridium flare: Satellites that used to momentarily catch the sun's reflection and shine brightly

L

law of attraction: A principle whereby feelings (vibration) and thought create manifestations
light body: A part of you that is energy that can travel independently from your physical body
Lion Beings: Advanced beings of feline and humanoid characteristics
lock on: When you signal a ship with a laser pointer or spotlight, and they signal back
low flier: a low flying UFO
lucid dreaming: Knowing you are dreaming, while you are dreaming

M

manifestation: The end result of creation through thought, word and action
mantra: Something you say over and over again to help you meditate or focus
meditation: Training the mind to focus, connecting to one mind consciousness
merging: Consensual blending with another being
merkabah: A divine light vehicle made with intention using sacred geometry
Military Industrial Complex (MIC): Unaccountable rouge arm of the U.S. government
military spacecraft: Ships made by humans reverse engineered from crashed UFOs
Milky Way: Stream of stars in a band across the sky, only visible in very dark areas
multi-dimensional: beings that can move between dimensions
mystery schools: organizations that hold and protect sacred teachings

N

namaste: "the divine in me greets the divine in you"
negative entities: annoying, scary, irritating but ultimately frivolous ghosts, spirits or energy
negative extraterrestrials: primitive other worldly beings that serve themselves
New World Order: An oppressive totalitarian system that the cabal has failed to put in place
non-physical beings: Spirits, ghosts, entities, etc. Any being that does not have a physical body
NORAD: North American Aerospace Defense Command
Nordics: Advanced beings similar to Caucasian humans in form
Northern Lights: Delightful natural light display occurring close to the poles

O

OCSETI: Okanagan Centre for the Study of Extra Terrestrial Intelligence
Om: A sacred mantra in Hinduism and Tibetan Buddhism meaning "the sound of the universe"
one mind consciousness: The hive mind, the collective consciousness, the limen etc.
orb: A moving sphere of energy and/or light, presenting in many sizes and colours
orientation: Understanding your position in a location (for CE-5s, under the heavens)
out of body experience (OBE): conscious awareness of when your spirit travels out of your body

P

parallel reality: A possible world or worlds that co-exists separately from ours
People's Disclosure Movement, The: An organization that promotes disclosure by the people
Pleiadians: Advanced beings similar to Caucasian humans in form
power-up: an orb of light or brightening that appears around a star, streaker, satellite, craft
pranic energy: Universal energy, life force, cosmic energy
probes: Little lights that visit close to the group that may be collecting information
protocol: A set way of executing a task
puja: Sanskrit song or prayer

Q

quantum mechanical: Physics theory of the behaviour of very small particles

R

Ranch, The: Nickname for ECETI
re-unification with source: Theory that all the separate parts of the universe will rejoin
remote viewing: A military process that collects information by accessing the hive mind
root chakra: Energy centre in the body at the base of spine/pelvis floor/genitals

S

sacral chakra: Energy centre at the lower abdomen below your navel
singing bowl: A Tibetan musical instrument that promotes deep meditation and relaxation
sky watch: Watching the skies for something, such as UFOs
slow walker: NORAD's term for an airplane
solar plexus chakra: Energy centre at the upper abdomen above your navel
Source: Another name for God, Creator, The Universe, Brilliant Pool of Infinity, etc.
space station on rings of Saturn: A space station reputed to be on the rings of Saturn
star being: Beings from the stars
star family: Another term for extraterrestrials, also referring to possible shared ancestry
streaker: A shooting star that might be a UFO
synchronicity: Not just coincidence – a universal aligning of circumstance

T

telepathy/telepathic communication: Using the mind to communicate/receive information
telomeres: DNA-protecting end caps at the end of chromosomes
theta brain state: When brain wave frequencies are slow, in meditation, relaxation, or sleep
third eye chakra: Energy centre just above and between your eyebrows

throat chakra: Energy centre at your throat

toning: Making a vowel sound for an extended period of time

trans-dimensional: Ability to move between dimensions

transcendental meditation (TM): A technique of meditation created by Maharishi Mahesh Yogi

U

UAP: Unidentified Aerial Phenomena

UFO: Unidentified Flying Object

universal law: Basic structure of how life works (i.e. We are all one, you get what you put out)

universal one: The alpha and omega, everything, all that exists

upgrade: Energy meant to heal or shift someone in a positive direction

V

vibration: The rate at which our elemental parts move, where high vibes = love, low vibes = fear

vortex/vortices: Special locations of heightened energy, or a mass of swirling energy

W

whistleblower: Someone who tells the illegal secrets of nefarious people or organizations

Z

zenith: The part of the sky directly overhead of you

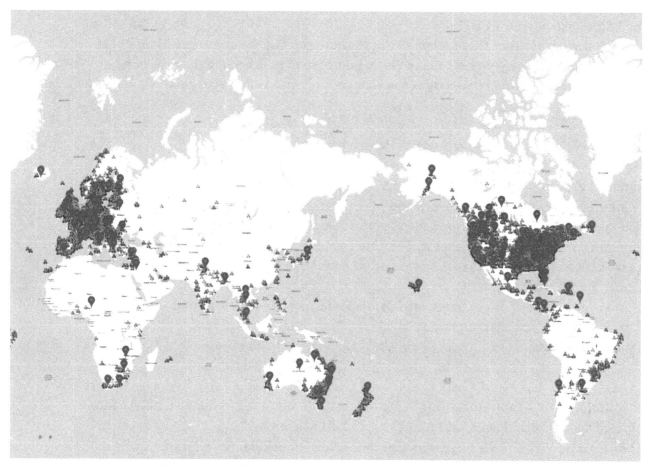

Registered members from both major CE-5 networking sites

INDEX

CPSIA information can be obtained
at www.ICGtesting.com
Printed in the USA
LVHW050718100820
662780LV00016B/517